THE
BLESSING
handbook

How to Give a Blessing
to Anyone Who Needs One

TERRY R. BONE

Table of Contents

Introduction

More than a decade ago I had an encounter with God's presence and grace that transformed the way I think. Through this encounter I learned how to discover and recover family blessings that I had missed growing up. It was like putting on a new pair of glasses. I suddenly realized how blurry my self-perception had been until then. Understanding and teaching this subject soon became a life pursuit.

As I designed and taught workshops, I observed that when people understand the power of blessing two questions typically surface:

- How can I receive the blessings I have missed?
- How do I give a blessing to someone else?

In our first book, *The Power of Blessing,* my wife Melissa and I focused more upon the first question. In this book, I am focusing upon the second.

I have structured this book in a "show and tell" format. In Part One, some chapters include step-by-step instructions, while others offer inspiring stories that paint a clear picture of what a blessing looks like in its various applications. Part Two includes samples and examples of written blessings from many real life applications. The results are awesome!

Once you've read this book, I trust you won't lay it aside to gather dust on the shelf. It is a guidebook and reference you can use time and time again to bless those you love.

I would like to begin that process by blessing you the reader:

May you be blessed by Your Heavenly Father as you read...

May He open the eyes of your heart to see...

May He give you a spirit of wisdom and revelation...

May you come to know the presence of God as you are blessed...

May you experience the power that can work through you as you bless others...

Terry R. Bone

PART ONE

Building a blessed life

CHAPTER I

The Power of Words

BLESSING! What an overused word!

When we are in good health we call it a blessing.

When an unexpected cheque comes in the mail, we call it a blessing.

When we enjoy an uninterrupted day, we call it a blessing.

When the policeman operating the radar gun catches the person speeding ahead of us, instead of us, we call it a blessing.

Whenever life is pleasing us in any way we call it a blessing.

So, you may ask, what is a real blessing? And what difference does it make in a person's life? An excellent short definition for blessing is "the empowerment to prosper."[1] In this context the word "prosper" doesn't refer to financial prosperity *per se*, but rather to our successfulness and ability to thrive in every area of life.

The first people on Earth, Adam and Eve, were blessed through God's words. These words became a divine "download" of essential affirmations that empowered them to thrive in their calling as "general managers" of the Earth. The difference the blessing made in their lives can easily be seen in the drastic changes that took place after the devil stole their blessing (see Genesis 3). Their relationship with God was immediately hampered by shame and fear. They lost their peace, and conflict entered their marriage. This conflict spread beyond them into all human relationships beginning with their own children Cain and Abel.

Today we see these same symptoms magnified in our family relationships. The conflict and lack of harmony that are so common in relationships today often result from the lack of blessings at the critical stages in life. Until we receive those blessings, we are also left without satisfactory answers to major life questions such as:

- Am I welcome in this World?
- Where is a safe place for me?
- Will my needs be met?
- Who can I trust?
- Do I have what it takes to make it?
- What am I called to do in this world?
- Who will share my journey?

If these questions remain unanswered, we strive for meaning and purpose. Our emotional energy is drained and our self-confidence is undermined. When the blessing is present, it empowers us because it delivers God's unique answers to these vital questions. Until we receive those blessings, we struggle to determine our true identity and destiny. As we receive the answers that blessing provides, our hearts are put at rest and we cease striving. (These questions are explained in greater detail in our book and DVD series *The Power of Blessing* – see Additional Resources for more info).

God most often chooses to impart the blessing we require through people. Two people in particular have the prime responsibility for delivering them as we grow up – our parents!

The unfortunate truth is that a majority of parents are not fully aware of how vital the blessing is, nor do they understand how to give this gift to their children. We haven't been schooled in the subject, nor do we have living models close to us to give us a picture of how it's done. As a result, many of us have never been given the blessings we were meant to receive. The good news is that it is never too late to recover missed blessings! The amazing thing is how quickly a person can move from surviving life to thriving in life once their missed blessings are appropriated. I have seen this happen countless times in the lives of people to whom we have ministered.

Through the stories in this book we hope to give you a clear picture of the impact of blessing on our closest relationships and beyond. Through this book you will learn how to impart blessing. We offer specific steps on crafting an effective blessing, and a plethora of examples and sample blessings.

So let's get started!

It all begins with understanding the power of words. In fact, everything in this world began with the power of words. Eons ago there was no physical world as we know it today. No material thing existed. No people, animals or physical life of any kind. There was no Earth and no solar system to hang it from; not one of the billions of stars, and no sky in which to view them.

And then a power was exerted that changed it all. God spoke, and a billion stars were flung into space. God spoke, and our solar system appeared. God spoke, and the ball of mud we call Earth became the home for millions of exquisitely designed forms of life. In fact, the first chapter of Genesis records God speaking at least 15 times using words to fashion and shape every aspect of life on Earth. You could say that using the spoken word was God's *modus operandi* for creation.

From this account we come to understand that words have *creative* power. But there's still more – words also have *staying* power. In fact God's words have eternal nature.

The prophet Isaiah declared, "The grass withers and the flowers fall, but the Word of our God stands forever" (Isaiah 40:8 NIV).

Whenever the Bible records God speaking, things begin to shift and people are affected; promises are given, destinies are declared, bodies are raised from the dead and mountains are moved. God's words have creative power and eternal nature.

God chose to share this power with only one facet of His creation – humankind. God's words gave each animal life; Adam's words gave them identity. Through words the devil challenged God's authority and eventually deceived Adam and Eve. Through words God promised them a way of redemption. Through words Jesus revealed the mysteries of the unseen kingdom of God and commanded a dead man to be raised. Through words the apostles preached the Gospel that changed the world in which they lived.

Your words have power as well! Death and life are in the power of *your* tongue (see Proverbs 18:21). The words you speak blaze a trail through the hearts and lives of those around you. Through words you can demolish a person's sense of self-worth or build in them an unshakable confidence.

Words affect us all from the time we draw our first breath. As we grow through childhood we form our worldview and self image largely from what has been spoken to us especially by our parents. When children trust the words to be true, the words write a message upon their hearts that in turn form a life "script" or belief system which they continue to follow into adulthood.

The influence of parents' words in shaping a child's belief system is powerfully illustrated in the life of Tiger Woods.

Before Tiger was 25 years old, he was well on his way to becoming recognized as the greatest golfer in history. A lot of it had to do with the words his father Earl Woods spoke to Tiger concerning his confidence in him. Earl claimed that he "knew Tiger was special the day he was born" and said that his goal was not to raise a golfer, but to raise a good person.[2] Tiger's success started extremely early. At the tender age of two he appeared on national TV demonstrating his putting skills with Bob Hope! Earl constantly encouraged and coached his little "phenom." By the age of four Tiger was achieving average adult scores and at 18 years of age he became the youngest amateur golf champ in American history.

When Tiger turned pro, Earl declared that his son had the mental toughness to become the most famous athlete on the planet. At the age of 21 Tiger shot a record 18 under par to win the Masters – the "crown jewel" of golf tournaments. Since then he has added nine more major tournament wins to his achievements and pretty well fulfilled his father's words.

Earl did his best to permit Tiger to develop his love for golf on his own, but never allowed his son to swing the clubs before he finished his homework. Meanwhile, Dad was always watching, teaching and proclaiming to all who would listen, the greatness he saw in his son. When Tiger met Nelson Mandela, Earl proudly spouted to the press, "It was the first time Tiger met a human being who was equal to him." We can forgive Earl for such obvious hyperbole when we look at the results. Rarely has a father so deliberately and thoroughly written a winning script for his son.

It is likely that most children have received less affirmation in their entire childhood than young Tiger Woods received in an average year. And many have not only missed the joy of affirmation, but have had to combat the pressure of negative or careless words.

How about you? Have you experienced an absence of affirmation? Perhaps you know someone who feels like they have been dumped at the doorstep of adulthood still carrying unanswered major life questions. Perhaps someone you love is still carrying an emotional wound caused by careless or negative words. Words of blessing can deliver vital affirmation and answer these essential questions. Words of blessing can heal those wounds!

God can use your words to help empower others to prosper! Through the power of words, you can become a courier who delivers life changing truth to the door of someone's heart. You can craft a blessing that will download heaven's resources into the life of someone you love. To quote a famous hardware store slogan – "You can do it...we can help!"

But as you learn the ways of blessing from this guidebook, please keep in mind that it's difficult to give something that you haven't first received. For blessing to flow *from* your life, it first needs to flow *into* your life. Be open to the work of the Holy Spirit to bless you so that the blessings you give will be as effective as they possibly can be.

Truth to go
Take a moment to pause and reflect...
- What were some words spoken to you that impacted your life as a child?
- Have any of these words caused you to believe something about yourself that is negative?

If you answered yes, you may want to pray this prayer...

"Heavenly Father, I open my heart to your Spirit. Please replace what I believe about myself with your truth as I learn the power of blessing."

---

[1] Thanks to Craig Hill, founder of Family Foundations International for this excellent definition see Additional Resources for contact information.

[2] Earl Wood's quotes appear in Christine Brown's article, "Tiger Loses His Favorite Driver," USA Today page 5B, Friday May 5, 2006.

CHAPTER 2

The Heart of Blessing

Years ago I worked in the computer division of a very successful airline. The atmosphere was frenetic, and success was measured by whether that day's flights left the runway on time, full of passengers. The managerial staff consisted entirely of high energy and high performance people. More often than not, the stress was clearly reflected on their faces, with one notable exception – a vice president named Kim. He was always calm and remained unperturbed in spite of the frequent mayhem around him. Kim's composure was rooted in his identity. It was derived not from his role in the company, but from his relationship with the owner of the company, who happened to be his father! The financial success and security that other managers strove to achieve through their work performance, were already Kim's as a gift. He was grateful to be the favored son of a kind father who would inevitably give him a rather large inheritance.

This story illustrates a spiritual truth concerning blessing. Blessings on your identity and destiny cannot be understood apart from a relationship with the "Father heart" of God. Your heavenly Father desires that you receive these spiritual blessings as a gift. However, some parents are unable or unavailable to deliver spiritual blessings to affirm their children's lives for a variety of reasons. As a result the children, in spite their talents and efforts, carry an emotional deficit into adulthood that only the missed blessing can fill.

That's exactly what happened to a young man named Doug. He now serves the Lord in fulltime Christian ministry, yet there was a time in his life when Doug's destiny was in question because of a missed blessing. Here's the story in his own words:

My Father died in Vietnam when I was five years old. The last thing I expected was to receive a letter from him 17 years later. But that is what happened one winter day when I was 22 years old.

It was the day my fiancée and I announced our engagement. My mom was overjoyed at the news, as was my stepfather. Such an event is a milestone for the mother of an only son, [and on this day] it occurred to her that I had become a man. That realization sparked in her the memory that years ago she had been given a solemn duty to discharge.

I remember being in the kitchen alone that evening. My mother walked in and handed me a letter copied onto old mimeograph paper, the likes of which I had not seen since kindergarten. The seven pages were still folded, evidence of an envelope since discarded.

'What's this?' I asked. 'It's something I should have given you years ago,' my mother said. 'It's a letter from your father. He wrote it to you from Vietnam soon after he arrived there, just in case something was to happen to him. He said that if he were not to return from the war, I was to give it to you when you became a man.... I realize that I should have given it to you a long time ago. I'm sorry.'

It is hard to describe how jolting her words were. My face paled. I went a bit numb. My hands turned cold and began to tremble slightly. I took the letter and went to my room. There's just something confusing about receiving a letter from your deceased father who has been gone so long that you have not one solitary memory of him. What I knew about him I had learned from asking questions of my mother, my grandmother and my aunts. I had read newspaper clippings and looked through scrapbooks. I had made peace with the fact that these tidbits were as much as I would ever know about my dad. There was no reason to expect more...certainly no reason to expect a personal letter

*seventeen years after a land mine ended his life.
I sat there in my room stunned. Finally, after a few
minutes, I managed to unfold the pages. They were
hand written. It felt like a privilege to see his hand-
writing. I had not seen it before.
Part of me was afraid to read it . . . afraid that – with
one quarter of my life behind me – I would find it
would not have pleased him...that I would not have
his blessing.... I had adjusted to not having to take into
account my father's approval or disapproval. Now, all
of a sudden, I might have to.
At the same time, I felt humbled that I was even get-
ting the chance to know my father's thoughts. How
many other boys, I wondered, would have this opportunity to read a letter from a father they never knew?"
The words took on an almost sacred quality to me.
This is part of what I read:*
'Dear Doug:
'Your old man is writing this letter tonight because he
feels the urge to share some basic thoughts with his
only son. You are a very little boy at this writing, but
the years will pass rapidly and someday soon you will
be a young man facing the realities of life.
'I fully expect to be around in the years to come and
hope to assist you on your path through life; however, one never knows what the future will bring.
'...Someday, you will have to decide on a career. Many
well-meaning people will offer their sincere advice and
you will undoubtedly be quite confused. The choice of
your life's work is equally as important as choosing a life's
mate. Before you can do either, you must decide what you
are yourself, as a person. As the years go by, you will soon
discover whether you are outward or timid, adventure-
some or docile, ambitious or complacent. It is no sin to
be one or the other; but it is extremely important that you
discover what you are – not what at some moment in life
you may think you would like to be.
'After you decide what you are – think about what you

*would like to be within the personality and innate intelli-
gence you possess – and then, unless you lack all ambition,
pick a goal several steps higher than what you think you
can achieve and work like the very devil to achieve it.*

*'Doug, you are a very intelligent boy and you have an
extremely kind disposition. Should something happen
to me... do not try to emulate a way of life that may
not be suitable to your own particular make-up. I do
hope you will choose a way of life that holds some
potential for helping to make this a better world...*

*'Ten years from now, let's you and I sit down and dis-
cuss this far too wordy letter...and learn from each
other, as I am sure that by then there will be much
your old dad can learn from you.*

'Love, Dad'

*When I finished reading the letter, it was as if the
weight of the world had been lifted from my shoulders.
I was not faced with trying to rebuild my life, after all.
Instead, my dad had affirmed me, citing traits he had
seen in me even when I was a little boy. His words
were encouraging and motivating, not scolding or dog-
matic. He did not lecture or warn me, but simply
shared his thoughts. Instead of trying to persuade me
to follow in his footsteps (which I had begun to do –
even applying to West Point, only to withdraw my
application), he held up virtues for which I could strive
no matter what career I chose. It felt good that, after
all those years, I had some basis for thinking my dad
would have been proud of me.*

*His letter had filled a place in my heart which I had only
been semi-aware of and had no idea was so large. I had
received my father's blessing... This man was a virtual
stranger to me, even though I shared his genes. Yet,
because he was my father, his attention and affirmation
in a letter mailed a week before his death profoundly
impacted the course of my life as an adult. He gave me
permission to proceed in a direction I would have gone
anyway, but now could go with greater confidence.*

It is my wish that every father would realize the innate and powerful impact he has upon his kids' lives...the potential he can endow toward self-esteem or self-hatred; toward confidence or insecurity. It is my wish that fathers would never miss a chance to plant seeds of encouragement in young hearts....[1]

Doug's story provides a poignant picture of a father who was determined to bless his son regardless of what occurred in the future. However, very few people can expect to recoup missed blessings from beyond the grave. Besides, the blessing deficit most of us suffer is not the result of untimely death. Rather it originates from an inability or unwillingness on the part of our parents to grant the gift of blessing that God intended for them to bestow upon us. What should we do?

Fear not beloved. God isn't sitting in heaven wringing His hands, looking at His angels with a wrinkled brow and moaning: Oh my goodness! This is a tough situation. What do we do now? Anyone up here have any ideas?

On the contrary God always has a plan that takes into account every facet of our current circumstances (see Ephesians 1:11-12).

Before you were born, our heavenly Father reviewed all the coming triumphs and tragedies of your life and fashioned a perfect plan to ensure that His blessing would still be available to you. I not only believe this, but know it to be true from experience. My own father died suddenly when I was a young adult. He didn't leave behind a letter. Even if he had been warned of his impending death, he wouldn't have known what to write.

But God had already devised a plan to ensure that the undelivered blessing would eventually reach the door of my heart. God allowed two people whom I knew and loved to perceive my need and deliver much of the blessing on my father's behalf. I also learned how to hear the voice of my heavenly Father directly through His Holy Spirit. I can honestly say today that I am thankful for the deficit that

God permitted in my life. It was key in motivating my search that led to the life-changing revelation I share with you in this book.

You and I have the same heavenly Father. He desires to bless you and He wants you to receive every blessing stored up for you in heaven's warehouse (see Ephesians 1:3) If you sense a deficit in the blessing department in your life, then know this fact – God is already waiting to unfold a plan that will more than make up for your lack. You can also be sure that His plan extends beyond your own need. He wants to use you to help make up that deficit in someone else's life.

As you read the rest of this handbook, be prepared for the Holy Spirit to highlight how He wants to bless you and use you to bless others.

Truth to go
Take a moment to pause and reflect: do you, or someone close to you, have an emotional deficit due to missed blessing?

Prayer for receiving:
Dear heavenly Father: I know that all blessings ultimately flow from you regardless of who brings them into my life. I lift up the following unmet need for blessing in my life: _____, and I ask you to unleash your plan for filling that need with your truth. Grant me the spiritual hunger and humility to persevere until all deficits have been erased by the power of your blessing.

Prayer for giving:
Dear heavenly Father, I want to be used to help erase the blessing deficit in the life of _____. Grant me the wisdom to know how and when to begin that process, and grant him/her the grace to perceive their need and receive the missed blessing through me or anyone else whom you would choose to use.

CHAPTER 3

Words, Deeds and Ceremonies

The Bible tells us that we have already received every blessing in Christ Jesus: "Praise be to the God and Father of our Lord Jesus Christ, who *has blessed us* in the heavenly realms with *every spiritual blessing* in Christ" (Ephesians 1:3 NIV – emphasis mine).

However, these blessings are sitting in heavenly realms like undelivered packages in a warehouse. You can believe the above verse, but how do you receive those blessings?

We have already established that God uses people to deliver His blessings to our lives. Now we will look at the means of delivery: words, deeds and ceremonies. Each of these contributes an important dimension to the process:

Words say it!
Deeds show it!
Ceremonies seal it!

When these three elements are intentionally entwined together, they become like the three-fold cord mentioned in the Bible that cannot be broken (see Ecclesiastes 4:12).

Words say it
We have already noted the ability of words to bless. I would take it a step further: a blessing cannot be given without words. God instructed Aaron to bless the people of Israel by speaking to them: "The Lord said to Moses, 'Tell Aaron and his sons, This is how you are to bless the Israelites. Say to them...'" (Numbers 6:22-23 NIV).

In fact, to pronounce blessings was one of the three main

purposes of the Aaronic priesthood: "...for the Lord your God has chosen them (the priests) to minister and *to pronounce blessings* in the name of the Lord and to decide all cases of dispute..." (Deuteronomy 21:5 NIV).

The word "pronounce" carries the connotation of authority. When a judge pronounces a sentence upon a prisoner, his words establish a new reality for that person's life. His words can also release a prisoner to freedom. In the same way, words of blessing carry authority in the spiritual realm. When a blessing is pronounced it establishes new liberty in a person's life.

The original language in this passage reveals that the authority inherent in a spoken blessing flows from God's partnership with the words. In Hebrew the phrase, "pronounce blessings," literally reads "bless by their word and the Lord." Effectively God was saying, If you will speak, I will act. God promised to partner with the priests' words to accomplish His spiritual activity in the lives of His people.

This principle is not limited to Old Testament priests. It is a universal principle of blessing that I have witnessed on countless occasions. When a person speaks words of blessing, the Holy Spirit is present to write those words upon the recipient's heart. Many times those present at a blessing ceremony can sense His presence when this occurs.

Deeds show it

The second strand in the cord is deeds. A deed is defined as an intentional action that is performed, or accomplished; an exploit or achievement.[1]

Deeds make our words more acceptable and believable. Actions that agree with our words add weight and credibility to what we say. Preparing a meal to accompany a formal blessing ceremony, purchasing or making a special gift, performing an act of kindness – these are but a few among many possible deeds that demonstrate the truth of the blessing we have spoken.

One of the ways I reinforced blessing with our children was to take each one on an outing that they would enjoy.

I used these special events as a backdrop to speak words of blessing. For example, as soon as my daughter Jessica reached school age, I began to take her on "dates with Daddy." The purpose of these dates was to communicate her value as a woman.

The date usually began with me leaving the house and returning to pick her up in a borrowed car – usually something much nicer than my own (preferably a convertible). After dinner and a movie, or mini-golf, or a walk in a park, Jessica would often share her dreams for the future. Throughout the evening I took every opportunity to convey respect and honor, even through little things like opening doors for her.

As we returned home, I gave her an informal verbal blessing that concluded with words like these: "You are an extremely bright and valuable person. You are the apple of your father's eye. You were placed upon this earth by God for a great and awesome purpose. Don't ever give your heart to a man who treats you with any less honor or respect than I have treated you today." At that moment those words had considerably more impact than if I had merely spoken them around the dinner table.

Another action that reinforces blessing is prayer. Although praying for someone to be blessed is not the same as blessing that person, prayer is a very important action that reinforces blessing. It plays an important supporting role. Prayers spoken with faith and accuracy condition the spiritual atmosphere around those we love, making it easier for them to believe and receive God's provision in every aspect of their lives.

Back to our opening analogy: if blessings are like packages delivered to the door of a person's heart, then prayer can clear the pathway upon which those blessings travel. Your prayers help to clear any spiritual "traffic jams" between heaven and the lives of the ones you love. Your prayers also help to ensure the enemy does not snatch the truth of God which has been deposited in their hearts.

Ceremonies seal it

God commanded the Israelites to gather together several times a year and conduct ceremonies to mark special occasions. These special occasions included three feasts (see Leviticus 23). During these celebrations work ceased and people gathered together to carry out purposeful, deliberate activities that reinforced their national identity and the message of God's faithfulness.

Unfortunately, our current culture has largely lost the connection between ceremony and celebration. For many of us the word "ceremony" is a pseudonym for boring, meaningless ritual. In fact one definition for ceremony I found actually lists the meaning as "any formal act or observance, especially a meaningless one."

A blessing ceremony is quite the opposite. When thoughtfully planned and orchestrated, it adds a visual dimension to the process that "seals" the meaning of the spoken words. Wedding ceremonies, graduations, anniversaries, special birthdays and rites of passage, such as the beginning of teen years, are obvious times when ceremonies can help instil a blessing that lasts a lifetime. Ceremonies can form family traditions that enable the blessing to endure and grow.

Ceremonies do not have to be restricted to formal occasions. For example, in our family we have adopted the practice of a New Year's blessing. During the last week of the calendar year, I ask God for Scripture passages that reflect His thoughts for each of my children for the coming year. Next, I craft words to go along with the truth to be applied to their lives. At some point we gather together in the family room. With the children seated, I lay my hand on each child's head one at a time while I pronounce their blessing. Melissa adds her words of agreement and additional insight. I record these blessings in my journal so that the following year we can review God's faithfulness in performing His Word in our lives.

Blessed be the tie that binds

Our New Year's blessing is just one variation on a theme. Families that take time to combine words of blessing creatively with deeds and ceremonies will soon find themselves forming enduring family traditions. They will discover that using a three-fold cord of words, deeds and ceremonies truly binds a family together in a healthy way.

Truth to go

Take a personal inventory. Ask yourself, What needs to change in my lifestyle to permit the three-fold cord of blessing to be woven together in my life?

- Words: Are there unspoken words of blessing in your heart for family or friends? Who in your circle of family and friends would be open to receiving a spoken blessing from you?
- Deeds: What deeds could you perform that would reinforce a needed blessing in the life of someone you love?
- Ceremonies: Are there any special occasions in the near future to which you could add a blessing ceremony?
- Prayer: For a sample prayer of protection, see Part Two, Section C.

[1] Deed. (n.d.). Dictionary.com Unabridged (v 1.1). from Dictionary.com website: http://dictionary.reference.com/browse/deed

CHAPTER 4

How to Craft a Blessing

In Genesis 49 we read the account of how Jacob blessed his sons and grandsons who eventually became the patriarchs of the 12 tribes of Israel. You will notice that each blessing consisted of two parts. Jacob spoke to each child individually about his character and his future. Each blessing was carefully crafted for the specific child to whom he was speaking. Under the guidance of the Holy Spirit Jacob outlined their unique identity and destiny one by one.

Similarly, to bless someone effectively you must have insight into their character and be able to perceive the positive future that God intends for them. This insight comes through a combination of relationship and revelation. When you deliver a spoken blessing, your goal is to recognize and verbalize the noteworthy characteristics of the recipients, and to articulate what you perceive God desires to do in their life and through their life in the future.

Perhaps you don't feel as self-confident as Jacob appears to have been when he eloquently blessed a dozen descendants on a single occasion. Often people who are not yet experienced at delivering a written or spoken blessing have a fear of making a mistake. That's understandable. But even a poorly delivered blessing is far better than no blessing at all. The truth is that whenever you attempt to give someone a blessing, God agrees with your efforts. The Holy Spirit partners with your blessing to bring results that often go beyond your own words.

The five elements of a blessing

We have discovered a format that works well for any kind of blessing. It's from a book entitled *The Blessing* by Gary Smalley and John Trent (see Additional Media Resources, page 106). In it, they outline five elements of a blessing:

19

- a meaningful touch
- a spoken message
- attaching a high value
- picturing a special future
- an active commitment

Each of these elements is flexible according to the situation. Let's review each one briefly:

A meaningful touch may range from a handshake to a big "bear hug," depending on the relationship between the participants and the occasion. Something powerful is communicated when a hand is laid upon the person being blessed. When we bless our children, I usually like for them to sit while I lay my hand on their head. The "laying on of hands" is also an important component during public blessing ceremonies.

A spoken message is the main substance upon which the blessing is built. A spoken blessing is more powerful when it is succinct. Write the text ahead of time so that you are confident that it reflects everything you wish to say concisely and clearly. It can be either in point form or verbatim. When it is time to pronounce these words, make direct eye contact with the person. You may first offer a few introductory words. Then, begin the blessing with phrases such as these:

I bless the following characteristics in your life...
May you be like (name a person), who was (name the characteristic)...

I see God at work in your life in the following way...

If you cannot speak to the person directly, or face to face, your blessing can also be effective delivered in written form.

Attaching a high value is a key component with which to begin a blessing. What do you see about the person's character that is worthy of praise? Your verbalization of

20

the person's value, and the value you place upon your relationship with them, is a powerful tool for the Holy Spirit to use in counteracting lies and depositing truth deep into a person's heart.

Picturing a special future involves comprehending through observation and insight what God desires to do in and through the recipient's life. Insight comes through relationship and revelation. This point is especially important for parents to note. Only when parents have a clear understanding of the potential of their child, can they pronounce a blessing with confidence and authority. When preparing a blessing, be sure to ask God to give you insight regarding the person's future.

An active commitment refers to your commitment to your future relationship with the person. It is probably the most flexible aspect of the blessing. When a commitment is verbalized during a public blessing ceremony it becomes a promise. Words of commitment ought to be carefully planned beforehand and not spoken in the emotion of the moment. A promise of commitment made and broken can be damaging to the relationship and can weaken the effect of the spoken blessing. A safe way to express commitment is to indicate your availability to help and counsel whenever you are asked. Sometimes, however, an occasion warrants more than that. If you are not the one who will be following up with commitment toward the person after the blessing, then add a prayer asking God to provide the right person.

Using the five elements

A few years ago at a conference, after I taught on the subject of Family Blessing, one of the attendees was eager to speak to me. He wanted to bless his daughter on her wedding day and wasn't sure how to proceed. I gave him these five elements and encouraged him to use them as a skeletal structure to flesh out with his own creativity. A few weeks later I received the following response in an e-mail:

My wife and I arrived back in town yesterday evening after our daughter's wedding. The father of the groom and I took about seven minutes in the ceremony to give the Parental blessing. We followed the five elements outlined in The Power of Blessing book.

We first spoke words of value about both the bride and groom. We then pronounced our blessing. We laid our hands on their shoulder for our meaningful touch. Then, speaking from a prepared text approximately one paragraph in length, we each told them how we would partner with them on their journey to blessing.

Following that, we presented them with a study Bible which my son-in-law and I had picked out. I wanted it to be a Bible that would be used, so we chose The Living Translation in a study format. We had it imprinted, and while [we were] in the store a customer volunteered to write in the front in calligraphy.

It was powerful – emotional! Everybody, including the 15 lawyers present (my son-in-law is a lawyer) and the officiating minister, commented on the uniqueness and the impact of the blessing. Thanks, Terry, for your help. What you shared really provided the framework for what we did...

I suppose I could say that this story proves the power of blessing. After all, 15 lawyers can't be wrong at the same time! I rest my case!

Not every blessing requires a public ceremony, and mothers often play as much of a role as fathers in imparting blessing. In this instance I was impressed at how well the fathers had worked together to craft the details of this blessing. Whatever the occasion, I recommend that you build your blessing upon these five elements and adapt it to your unique situation.

The role of prayer

Remember that a blessing is not a prayer. Prayer ought to accompany a blessing, but it does not replace it. People who do not understand this will often revert to praying when asked to participate in a blessing ceremony. Typically, they bow their heads, close their eyes and ask God to bless the person for whom they are praying. Now don't get me wrong, that is a good thing to do. However, asking God to bless someone is not the same as giving them a blessing yourself! A blessing should be spoken in the first person using direct eye contact. Prayer may then play a role as part of the active commitment that follows.

Truth to go

If you desire help with the wording of a blessing, you can review the samples and examples found in Part Two of this book. Then make a copy of, "A Blessing for Someone I Know," found on pages 80-81 and follow these steps:

- Prayerfully choose a Scripture that conveys a positive message suitable to the person you wish to bless. Hint: Look for ones that start with the phrase "May you..." or "May God..."
- Write a sentence or two describing something note-worthy that you have observed about this person's actions or character.
- Record words that describe this person's value in your eyes and in the sight of God.
- Add any good thing that you perceive God to be doing in their life right now.
- Describe the ways in which you believe this person can be used by God to encourage and bless others in the future.
- If appropriate, state how you are willing to assist this person to achieve the future you have pictured for them.
- Optional: Find the meaning of this person's name and incorporate it into the blessing (see Chapter 10).

CHAPTER 5

Learning from the Pros

When I teach a Family Blessing seminar, I often ask if anyone in the audience grew up in a family where blessings were spoken on a regular basis. *It's rare to see a hand raised in response.* In fact very few people I have met claim to have ever received such a blessing from their parents more than a few times in their entire childhood. Yet in an observant Jewish family most children experience blessing nearly a thousand times before they leave their parents' home! It's not hard to conclude that Jewish families are in a league of their own when it comes to Family Blessing. You could say they are "pros" on the subject!

Blessing is in the "DNA" of a Jewish family. Their physical existence is a direct result of God's promise to bless Abraham and to make his descendents a blessing to all families on Earth (see Genesis 12:1-3). Jewish identity is deeply rooted in the biblical account of the way in which Abraham's blessing was passed along from generation to generation in spite of many obstacles. Since that time, a faithful remnant of Jews has continued to pass this Family Blessing on to succeeding generations for more than 3,000 years.

The Sabbath blessing

One of the most well known expressions of the Jewish Family Blessing is the weekly Shabbat (Sabbath) blessing. It is spoken to children as part of a weekly ceremony that follows ancient tradition, yet leaves room for individual expression.

Here is an excerpt from a modern day guide:
There are many variations on how the blessing is made. The most common custom is for the father to put his hands on the child's head and recite the blessing. (In some homes the mother gives the blessing with the father, or even

instead of the father). The blessing may be followed by a kiss or personal words of praise. In some homes each child gets up at the table and stands before the parent to get the blessing, and in other homes the parent walks around the table and blesses each seated child, often praising some accomplishment in his or her week.

The blessing for a Son asks God to make them like Ephraim and Menashe. Why? Just before he dies, Jacob blesses his two grandsons, Ephraim and Menashe. He says they should become role models for the Jewish people in the future (see Genesis 48:20) Ephraim and Menashe did in fact become role models worthy of emulation. Unlike those before them, including Cain and Abel, Isaac and Ishmael, Jacob and Esau, and Joseph and his brothers, Ephraim and Menashe were not rivals. Rather, they were brothers united by their drive to perform good deeds. Also they were the only ones of the twelve patriarchs to grow to maturity outside the land of Israel, yet they remained steadfast.

The blessing for a Daughter asks God to make them like Sarah, Rebecca, Rachel and Leah. Why? Each of the matriarchs has qualities that qualify them to be role models.

The matriarchs were strong and laudable women. They endured difficult home lives, hardships in marriage, infertility, abduction, envy from other women, and difficulties with children. Nevertheless, these righteous women, through their individual passion, their partnerships with the patriarchs and their loyalty to God, succeed to build a nation.

Whatever procedure is followed, the blessing is sure to make the child feel special and loved, boost the child's self-esteem, and give the child fond memories of Shabbat family together time.[1]

One reason for the effectiveness of the Shabbat blessing over the centuries is that it is not limited to special occasions. It is ensconced in the Sabbath tradition which ensures that families observe it without fail on a weekly basis.

Another reason for its effectiveness is found in the manner in which the Sabbath is observed. It is a day filled with meaningful symbols, songs and prayers[2] – a marvellous blend of words, deeds and ceremonies woven into a three-fold cord that despite all attempts, could not be broken. Parents who are serious about creating a blessing legacy can learn much from this tradition. Regular family times set aside for celebration and blessing are a fundamental component. But because we live in a frenetic culture that has little or no appreciation for the value of Sabbath rest, creative methods may be required for gathering family members together on a regular basis. Those who persevere reap tremendous rewards.

A third reason for the success of the Shabbat blessing relates to the personal connection the Jews have with biblical figures from the past.

Out of curiosity one day I casually asked a Jewish friend, "Yaffa, where do you come from?" I expected her to respond with the city or region of her birth. Instead she turned to me with a puzzled look and exclaimed, "You have read the Bible and you don't know the answer? Why, I come from Abraham, of course!"

Yaffa's response highlights a significant truth. The Jewish people have a connection with their roots that is completely foreign to most Gentiles (the biblical term for non-Jews).

Jewish people read the Old Testament like a family journal, and indeed it is. As Gentiles we miss out because we don't identify with the biblical figures as our personal ancestors. However, through faith in Christ we can all lay claim to the spiritual blessings given to Abraham's descendants (see Romans 4:16). Any parent can invoke the qualities of biblical characters for their children through a spoken blessing. Melissa and I intentionally named our first child David after the biblical hero King David. We have often used his character qualities when forming a blessing for our son.

Connecting with your own heritage

While it is true that biblical heroes provide a rich source of character qualities from which we can draw, I also highly recommend that you search for "blessing material" within your own family heritage. Ancestral information is often no more than a curiosity for many of us. As a result we never find out about potential blessings that remain hidden like a can of preserves in the family cellar. When a person finally decides to investigate for themselves, it is surprising how often their research leads to the discovery of a "God story" in their family history. Here are two examples:

A minister named Bill attended a conference where I was speaking. He experienced an ongoing struggle with his sense of identity which was rooted in the reminders he constantly received that he was an "illegitimate child" – a terrible term from yesteryear for children who were born outside of marriage.

During the conference Bill received personal ministry that helped him recover the early life blessings he had missed. Following this, Bill researched his family history and, to his utter amazement, discovered in it more than 13 ministers of the Gospel whose lives spanned several previous generations. This discovery helped erase and replace the lie in Bill's heart that he was an accident. Now he clearly saw the truth that he was chosen by God to perpetuate a family calling to full time Christian ministry.

Another example comes from a church leader named Penny who listened to our teaching on the subject of generational blessing. A few months later she wrote us::

No one in my family knew the Lord, so it never dawned on me that I might have a godly heritage somewhere in my family line. One afternoon I asked my mom if we had any people of faith in our family history. Lo and behold, she replied, yes; I had a cousin who was a pastor and second cousins who were missionaries. There was also a Baptist minister, and even my grandmother had taught Sunday school before I was born. I did have a godly heritage in my own blood line! That knowledge in itself was a tremendous blessing to me.

Like Penny and Bill, I also used to believe that I didn't have a spiritual heritage to celebrate. One day after I expressed that opinion in public, I felt a strong rebuke from the Holy Spirit. In my mind I heard the words, "Stop that! You are dishonoring Me." I decided to research what I had assumed was a fairly barren spiritual history. To my surprise I discovered hints of a rich heritage that included ancestors who were named after John Wesley, the great English revival preacher and founder of Methodism. Around the same time a "chance" meeting led me to discover that our church was near the site of an historical Methodist revival movement during a period of time when my ancestors lived in the same region. These findings uncovered for me a new aspect of my true identity and destiny. My new-found connection with my spiritual heritage profoundly impacted the way I think about myself. I sense a personal connection as I read the history of the Methodist movement. I also have a new level of confidence with which to bless my children. Now when I lay my hands upon them, I invoke the generational blessing that is upon our family line.

Starting your own traditions

Regardless of whether you discover any significant facts about your spiritual heritage from generations past, you yourself can begin a spiritual heritage that outlives you and lasts for generations to come. Do not minimize the value of simple family rituals that can be used as a platform for family blessing. In an article on how to successfully parent pre-teens and teens, psychologist Michael Thompson says: "Keep up the family rituals that have always sustained you: family dinners, church, camping, skiing and watching the same dumb TV shows. (Children) need to feel that ...they can be nourished by traditions they know well."[3]

With a little forethought and planning any parent can turn certain aspects of the family routine into an opportunity to form a blessing tradition.

Truth to go

- Discover your heritage: Fill out the family tree chart found on page 79. Trace your family lineage beyond the chart. List anything positive you discover about your family's spiritual heritage.

- Pray the following generational blessing prayer and see what God reveals:

  "In the name of Jesus I reach back in faith and call forward my spiritual heritage in Jesus Christ purchased by His blood on the cross. I receive into my life every provision that the Father God intended for me and my family line. I receive the full measure of God's purpose for my generation and my descendants. I call for every spiritual blessing from past generations that has not yet been fully released, to be transferred into my life. I ask You Lord to reveal and release the full spiritual power that is available to me on this basis. – In the Name of Jesus, Amen."

- Establish a Family Blessing: Examine your family schedule. What do you need to change so you have time to give blessings to your children regularly? What could you incorporate into a regular Family Blessing event? Which biblical characters could you use in crafting a blessing?

[1] Adapted from *Blessing the Children* by Lisa Katz ©2007
http://judaism.about.com/od/sabbathdayshabb2/qt/bless_children.htm.
Used with permission from About, Inc. online at www.about.com.
All rights reserved.

[2] Here are a few examples, courtesy www.aish.com:
Amidah – The silent prayer said as part of every prayer service.
Eishes Chayil -- "The Woman of Valor," a song in praise of the Jewish woman, written by King Solomon. Traditionally sung Friday night.
Bentching (Yiddish, meaning "to bless") Grace recited at the conclusion of the three meals.
Challah – Bread traditionally used on Shabbat, often braided. Literally, challah is a mitzvah in the Torah (see Numbers 15:17-21), which enjoins us to set aside one piece of dough from each batch we make, as it says: "...It shall be that when you eat the bread of the land, you shall set aside a portion for God."

[3] Michael Thompson, "What They Won't Tell You, and Why," *Time Magazine*, August 8, 2005 , 49.

CHAPTER 6

Pre-Birth to Early Childhood

A spoken blessing is the biblical means for transferring God's favor from one generation to the next. The promise God made to Abraham would have failed to materialize if Isaac and Jacob had not blessed their children and grandchildren. In the Gospels, we see Jesus setting the example. Not only did He bless little children who were brought to Him (see Mark 10:16), but Scripture records that Jesus Himself was blessed on at least three occasions by the time He was a very young child (see Matthew 1, Luke 1 and 2).

Families today can expect outstanding results when they follow these examples of blessing throughout each stage of a child's life.

The pre-born stage

When Mary conceived Jesus and knew she was "with child," she hurried to the house of her older relative Elizabeth. Elizabeth was in the midst of her own miraculous pregnancy which resulted in the birth of John the Baptist. She blessed both Mary and her pre-born Saviour. You can read about this wonderful meeting of the mothers in Luke 1:26-56.

Every mother-to-be and her baby need blessing. It is rapidly becoming an established scientific fact that the emotions of a pre-born child are active and affected significantly by the mother's emotions. A Christian psychotherapist who attended one of our seminars corroborated this: "You mentioned the importance of blessing pregnant women... I actually wrote a research paper for the

Journal of Transactional Analysis entitled "The Secret Life of the Developing Embryo." You are right; there's heaps of research that proves that our life in vitro is profoundly affected by the emotions of the mother – and this can then affect the whole of our life..."

Melissa and I believe that pregnant women deserve to be honored with special treatment. What is happening in their bodies is miraculous and holy, and the "red carpet" should be rolled out for them. People who are in contact with an expectant mother ought to be willing to help reduce the physical and emotional stress she experiences during pregnancy. There's much that dads, friends and family can do with kind words and thoughtful deeds during this time that will increase the blessing the baby receives.

Spoken blessing is also valuable at this stage, and because an expectant mother and child are uniquely interconnected, it is important to bless both of them. Melissa describes how she leads a blessing for an expectant mom:

"I always ask permission first to see if the mother is comfortable to receive a blessing, especially if it is in front of others. I ask for both partners to be present if possible. I ask mom to put her hand on her tummy, then dad to put his hand on hers, then I put my hand over top of them both. Baby often moves during the blessing, just like John the Baptist did!

First I address the mom to bless her health during pregnancy and her labor and delivery. I ask God to make it stress-free and peaceful for them. I encourage the mother to write down what the Lord may be saying during her pregnancy about her child, its identity and destiny.

Then I speak directly to the baby. Depending on the trimester of the mother's pregnancy and the stage of gestation, I often bless what I know is taking place in the development of the baby. I finish the blessing by telling the child to "stay put" until the fullness of time – the day God has chosen for his/her birthday. In this way, both mom and baby are blessed." (For complete guidelines and wording of this Pregnancy Blessing see Part Two, Section B).

The newborn stage

A month after Jesus' birth, He was blessed on His first trip to the temple. God had specially prepared two seniors to recognize Him by the Spirit. During His dedication, both Simeon and Anna blessed baby Jesus and spoke prophetically about His identity and destiny.

The blessing at birth includes naming and dedicating (or baptising) the baby. Regardless of which tradition you follow, your faith as a parent is active rather than the child's faith. The baptism or dedication brings children under God's protection and activates the unfolding of God's plan for their lives. When Melissa and I served in pastoral ministry, we made a "big deal" out of baby dedications. They not only included the child's extended family but also the church family.

Before the dedication, I always interviewed the parents and asked them to prayerfully choose a life Scripture that would apply to their child as they grow. I requested that grandparents be present and involved, if possible, and encouraged the parents to include other members of the extended family as well. During the ceremony, the father, if present, recited the life Scripture and explained the reason it was chosen. Others had an opportunity to share what they felt God had laid upon their hearts for this child and the family. The parents also recited the typical vows to raise their child in a Christian home. They could tailor the wording to suit their own wishes, but the vows always included three promises:

- to teach and train the child with the principles of God's Word
- to seek to lead the child to a saving faith in Jesus Christ at an early age
- to provide godly examples by their own lives

To conclude the ceremony, I held the child in my arms, dedicated his/her life to the Lord and spoke any additional words of destiny I felt were prompted by the Holy Spirit (a sample dedication blessing is included in Part Two). This kind of ceremony is not restricted to newborns – it can also be performed for older children who have not yet had the privilege of receiving this blessing. It can be a profound experience for children old enough to understand the words being spoken.

The early years

Within two years of Jesus' birth Mary and Joseph received visitors called Magi. These important political persons made an arduous trek from a country east of Israel exclusively for the purpose of blessing the young toddler. The Magi recognized and honored Jesus' identity in His presence (see Matthew 2:11). The ceremony they conducted included the giving of gifts and a spoken blessing. Their words and actions illustrate the importance that the heavenly Father places upon blessing at this stage of life.

Spoken blessings are not to be limited to special occasions, but ought to be integrated into the regular family routine as well. The hearts of young children are quite vulnerable to the words of the significant adults in their lives. Parents of young children do well to remember that when they speak to their youngster, they are often writing upon the child's heart with their words.

Young children value consistency (read repetition). When our children were pre-schoolers, they asked for the same book to be read to them night after night. They loved the familiarity of the words. Rolf Garborg, in his book, *The Family Blessing,* tells a story of the impact a blessing he spoke over his two children every night for 20 years had on them. In one winsome anecdote he relates that when his daughter discovered he was leaving on a business trip for 30 days, she insisted on receiving 30 blessings the night before he left. When he had finally finished, she said, "You can go on your trip now daddy, everything's going to be okay."

The main elements of the nightly blessing that Rolf Garborg spoke over his children were simple yet profoundly effective. They included a Scripture, some personal words and a hug. Repetition built a secure foundation of trust. A daily blessing imprinted the practice deep within his children's souls.

It is not necessary to follow a precise formula or repeat the exact words every time. I suggest using a combination of prepared words (such as Numbers 6:24-26) and extemporaneous words – those that come to mind on the spur of the moment. This gives the Holy Spirit a chance to speak a timely word through you, while at the same preserving the repetitive routine that is reassuring to young lives. Bedtime is not the only time a blessing is welcome. Early morning and mealtimes can be favorites too.

Parents need to remember that words alone do not complete the job of blessing. Children also need a protected environment that is kept safe by trustworthy adults. "As a twig is bent, so grows the tree." Just as a small plant must be protected from being bent or broken, so the mind and heart of a young child needs to be protected from the negative influences that will damage their fragile sense of identity as they grow. Harsh words, anger, lack of physical touch, teasing or bullying are just a few examples of what I refer to as "blessing blockers." Another enemy of blessing is the practice of using shame as a motivator for correcting behavior. It is essential during these years that parents learn to train a child's will through loving discipline. They can do this by separating their child's value as a person from his/her behavior.[1]

Teaching children about blessing

The Bible tells parents that if they "train up a child in the way he should go, even when he is old he will not depart from it" (Proverbs 22:6 NASU).

Children need to learn about blessing. In the home, at church (and at school where permissible) even very young children can be instructed in the meaning of how to give and receive blessings.

A children's pastor I know developed unique ideas for blessing young children. She used the milestones of a child's first birthday and beginning first grade in school as back-drops for blessing celebrations. In her own words:

"In our children's ministry we take the time to celebrate this important milestone with families. We invite all the children who celebrated their first birthday the year before to a "Turning One" celebration along with their parents. We have a collective party for all these children. One year we rented 'inflatables' at the church, another year we did a stuffed bear party. This is a great chance to invest in these families spiritually – we give each child a toddler Bible and encourage parents to begin a devotional time together with their children. Then we pray and bless them and their families. It lets parents know that you value the life of their little one.

"Going into grade one is also a huge milestone in the lives of children that we like to celebrate. Starting full days of school can be hard for children (and parents) so blessing is especially welcomed at this stage. We normally take them to an indoor party place, and let them have a great time playing and having fun! Again, this is great relationship and connecting time for children and families. For this party, we bless each child with a back-to-school kit of school supplies, and we also get them a devotional book to start off their new school year. This makes them feel really special and again it is a spiritual investment into their lives. We pray over them, and this new season of their life. This has become a really special milestone event for the children in our church entering grade one!"

Parents and teachers can adapt these activities for use outside the church setting as well.

In another church the children's ministry leader devised a ten-week curriculum about blessing centered on a modern version of Numbers 6:24-26 and used the parts of body to communicate ways in which we need to be blessed. A blessing song and puppet skits were included. On the last week, there was a party at which every child received a written blessing to take with them (more details available at www.powerofblessing.com). Here is how that curriculum explains blessing to children:

> May the LORD bless you and protect you.
> May the LORD smile on you and be gracious to you.
> May the LORD show you His favor and give you His peace
> (Numbers 6:24-26 New Living Translation).

When you bless someone, you are asking God to do these five things. The blessing you offer will not only help the one receiving it, it will also demonstrate love, encourage others, and provide a model of caring for others.

A spoken blessing was one way of asking for God's divine favor to rest upon others. The ancient blessing in these verses helps us understand what a blessing was supposed to do. Its five parts conveyed hope that God would

- bless and protect them
- smile on them (be pleased)
- be gracious (merciful and compassionate)
- show his favor toward them (give his approval)
- give peace

I am not sure that I could think of a better way of explaining it to adults!

Truth to go

Take time to pause and reflect: Is there an unresolved issue that may hinder you from passing on Family Blessing to the next generation?

For parents:
- Have your children been dedicated or baptized? Have you discerned anything about God's direction for their lives that you can use in a blessing?
- Do you practice bedtime blessings? What may need to change in your family's lifestyle to allow for this or other regular blessing activities?

- How do you speak to your children? What is the ratio of positive to negative messages you give them?
- Is there a special occasion coming up in your child's life that could be used as a platform to deliver blessing?

---

[1] Correction without affirmation almost never brings positive results. One counselor I know teaches that a child typically needs to receive five positive messages for every one negative message to retain the intended blessing from parents.

CHAPTER 7

Rites of Passage at Teen Years

At key transition points in each of our lives we must stop and address the questions, Who am I? and Where am I going? Our life's journey can be delayed until we provide satisfactory answers to these questions.

One of the most challenging transitions occurs at the "border crossing" from pre-teen to teen years. As a teenager's body attains sexual maturity, his or her mind begins to grasp for a new identity.

For centuries many cultures have addressed this transition by developing certain "rites of passage." In days gone by, a boy might have been required to perform great feats of skill in hunting or physical endurance to prove his manhood. Even today many cultures still employ ceremonies, most of which feature less exertion and more celebration. However, the purpose is the same – to mark the key transition from childhood to adulthood.

A Bar Mitzvah, which means "son of the commandment," or Bat Mitzvah, "daughter of the commandment," is completed by Jewish boys and girls between the ages of 12 and 14. When Jewish young people undergo their "Bar/Bat Mitzvah," they assume the responsibilities of an adult under Jewish law: they are no longer innocent, and become responsible for their own actions (good or bad). The celebrations can be extremely elaborate!

The Quinceañera or Quince Años (meaning "15 years") is still practiced today in Latin America. This celebration marks the transition from childhood to womanhood. Traditions include giving and throwing a quince doll which signifies the young lady's last doll as a child. She throws it to the other female children in attendance, much as a bride throws a garter at a wedding reception. After the inaugural dance, the girl sits in a chair in the center of the dance floor, and her father removes her flats ("girls" shoes). He then puts high heels on her feet, signifying her becoming a young lady.[1]

However, the value of imparting a special blessing to young teens has largely been ignored in Western culture. It is heartening, therefore, to see many Christian families today rediscovering the value and effectiveness of individually designed blessing events for their teens. This type of ceremony has become known to some as a Bar/Bat Barakah (son/daughter of blessing) ceremony, or a Christian Bar/Bat Mitzvah.

Three elements of a blessing ceremony
Whether these blessing events are simple or elaborate, they involve three basic elements:

First: A period of instruction
Planning of the event ought to begin well in advance. Key to its success is the child's understanding and ability to embrace its purpose. Just as a teen being confirmed in a church is required to attend confirmation classes, so parents need to take time to cover topics important in the child's life and future with respect to blessing. Craig Hill, in his guidebook for parents, says that instruction should prepare the child for five things:[2]

1. to enter into a settled sense of adult identity
2. to enter into a clear sense of purpose and personal mission statement
3. to be emotionally released into manhood or womanhood
4. to take responsibility for his/her own spiritual health
5. to walk in sexual purity all the days of his/her life

Second: The content of the ceremony
A uniquely designed ceremony typically includes the following:

1. an instructive word of encouragement from significant people in the child's life
2. a verbal/written commitment from parents to the ongoing process of life coaching
3. a response by the child reaffirming their commitment to the Lord, along with a promise to honor their parents and to pursue their destiny
4. an exchange of meaningful gifts such as a "promise ring" (from a father to his daughter) that represents her commitment to sexual purity

Third: The celebration

The ceremony is held in conjunction with a dinner, a party or other special event. It is advisable to include the child in planning so that the celebration reflects their desires.

Whatever form they may take, the common purpose of these ceremonies is to communicate value and worth, to affirm blessing on a child's gender, gifts and talents, and to call the child forth as an emerging adult.

Although ceremonies can leave a lasting impression, it is naïve to imagine that a single ceremony, no matter how elaborate, can fulfill the function of transitioning a young person from child to adult. Teens must answer the life question, *Do I have what it takes to make it in this world?* They will need continued encouragement throughout their adolescent years to adequately answer this question for themselves, and a blessing ceremony is just the beginning.

Ideas for parents

Rick, a friend of mine, designed beautiful events for each of his two daughters. Here is how he describes them:

On their 13th birthdays I took each of our girls out for an evening in a way that fit their interests. I took one to the highest end restaurant in the city. I took the other for the best wings and ribs in town followed by a night at the theatre. Both of them received a ring, (as expensive as I could afford without being too exces-

sive) to understand how valuable they are and how important their purity is to the heart of God. Once it was placed on their finger, it was not to come off until their wedding day (and so far it hasn't). I ensured that they fully knew before the night began what was coming, and were ready and wanting to make the commitment.

Then we also had individual blessing parties for each of them. It isn't a blessing if it doesn't connect with them, so I spent some time talking with my girls in advance introducing what we wanted to do and ascertaining what would make it spiritually significant for them. We found out who the people were in their lives that had made an impact on them from as early as they could remember to [the present], and invited as many as we could. I asked every person to prepare something to say that would bring the blessing of God to their lives.

Everything that was said was to be written out so that a scrapbook could be made for those days when the girls might question God's plan for their lives, as happens to all of us from time to time...(my one girl has a private drawer filled with words of encouragement and letters).

The meal was part of their plan as well...much like a birthday where they are the honored guest. One daughter wanted it all fancy and the other had a barbeque.... One dressy...one in blue jeans!

Jeff, another friend, planned a similar event for each of his two boys. He arranged with the school principal for his eldest son to be visited throughout the day by significant people in his life. He followed up this event with a special dinner during which a carefully selected group of ten men each spoke to the boy about a character trait of a godly man. Several of the guests also gave his son a meaningful gift or prayed for him.

Jeff planned a different kind of event for his other son.

He took him on a walk through places significant to him from his own childhood and shared stories and lessons from his life. After this intimate time of fellowship, Jeff had arranged for a dinner party. People significant in his son's life were invited to attend the event.

No more secrets

Even though a parent carefully designs a meaningful blessing ceremony, they may encounter roadblocks that prevent teens from receiving the required blessing. As the old saying goes – honesty is the best policy. It is also an essential building block for blessing. Parents often believe that they are "protecting" their children by shielding them from family secrets. Sometimes the motivation is to cover shame. But as a child approaches teen years, withholding the truth becomes an act of dishonor. As daunting as the task may seem in some situations, speaking the truth in love is a prerequisite for successfully delivering a blessing. One family I know experienced this in a profound way:

A married couple (whom I will call Brenda and Sam) approached me after a workshop to share a family secret. Seventeen years prior, Brenda had conceived a child through an extra-marital affair. She had confessed to her husband, and he had agreed to keep the child and raise her as his own. Now, at 16 years of age, this daughter looked physically different from her siblings and had never felt she belonged in the family. She was starting to demonstrate rebellious behavior that no amount of parental effort could overcome.

I told them that they could not build a house of blessing on a foundation of lies. Until the daughter, whom I will call Laura, was properly welcomed into their family based on her true identity, their attempts at blessing would be severely weakened. I recommended that they take her away for a weekend and during that time confess the truth.

Sam and Laura prayerfully followed through with this suggestion. They invited Laura to spend a weekend alone with them and allowed her to pick the location. She chose a mountainside retreat. Here's what happened in Brenda's words:

Our trip with Laura was one of the hardest things I have ever had to do. To sit there and tell my own daughter that I had had an affair and been unfaithful to her dad was not easy. Sam spoke to her first and told her what she meant to him. Then I read her a long letter listing all the things I love about her and how special God made her. I didn't realize how much love I had for her until that moment. We all cried and hugged and Laura listened very carefully. God gave us the words to say and the strength to tell her everything. Her first response was, "He's not my real Dad?" She appreciated our honesty and enjoyed the time alone with us. We both hugged and held her. She seemed relieved [because] she had known something was up, but now there was a peace in her spirit after we were finished talking.

I knew for years that God had forgiven me, but until Laura was aware of the truth, I had no idea that freedom could feel so wonderful.

Laura seems to be happier, and I am able to love her more than ever. She also is showing much more love for us. She made Sam a Father's Day card that brought tears to our eyes. She's going to be okay. God has set us free!"

Sam and Brenda did not stop there. They felt that God wanted them to bring this situation completely into the light, so with Laura's permission they invited the rest of the children to a family meeting. They honored Laura by including her in the event planning. The date was set to coincide with Brenda and Sam's 25th wedding anniversary. Here is what happened, again in Brenda's words:

...that evening after supper, we told the children that we were going to have a family talk. They were all a

bit nervous [because] they thought they were in trouble! I started off with verses from Ephesians which changed the mood. I told them that there was something their dad and I had kept from them, thinking it was the right thing. But now we realized that they needed to know. Sam explained to them what had happened and the role he played in it. He did an excellent job and I was so proud of him. The girls took it the hardest, and we made sure we let the kids know that Laura wanted them to know. We then asked them individually for forgiveness and each one of them lovingly responded with a 'Yes.' They were relieved at the fact that I didn't have to live with the lie anymore. They each went to Laura on their own afterwards and hugged her and said that she is their sister and nothing will ever change that. That was so good for Laura. I am so glad that there are no more secrets.

I wanted to know – did the blessing work? Had it produced lasting effects? I e-mailed Brenda more than a year later to find out, and here is how she replied:

... every time I reflect back to that time in my life, it shows me how great a God we have and how blessed our family really is; especially when everyday life isn't going so well. Laura is doing so much better. She has lots of friends and much joy...She is happy to be in our family. In this day and age there are too many secrets that are damaging lives that could be so happy. For us it was the right thing to do to share it with Laura and our other children. God will continue to bless us because of this.

Sam and Brenda abandoned their shame and discovered that "where sin increased, grace increased all the more" (Romans 5:20). May parents everywhere find the same courage to speak the truth in love so the blessing may be given.

Truth to go

Take time to pause and reflect.

- Are there any secrets in your family that may impede the giving and receiving of blessings? Do not allow shame or fear to keep you from bringing to light those situations that God's grace can turn into blessings.

- To learn more about the blessing during teen years, see chapter 12 in *The Power of Blessing* book and session #8 in the DVD series.

- Do you have children in their teen years who require a special blessing event? Ask God to give you insight regarding their unique gifting and calling in life. Then prayerfully plan the event using the examples and instructions in this chapter.

A special note to parents who have performed a Bar Barakah ceremony with their teens:

- If your children have already experienced their Christian "rite of passage" blessing, then maybe it's time to send them on a mission trip or get them involved in some form of outreach ministry where they can strengthen their newfound sense of identity by serving others.

[1] Excerpted from Wikipedia http://en.wikipedia.org/wiki/Quincea%C3%B1era

[2] Hill, Craig, Bar Barakah, A Parent's Guide to a Christian Bar Mitzvah. Family Foundations International, 1998, 39.

CHAPTER 8

Milestones – Young Adults to Seniors

It is not very difficult to find your way across North America by car today, especially if your vehicle is fitted with a GPS satellite guidance system. But long before the days of Google Earth and Mapquest, the ancient paths were marked with milestones strategically placed along well-traveled routes. Travelers required them to track their progress and to keep from losing their way.

Our life journey is also marked by "milestones." In fact this term has become a common metaphor for the significant events that mark the progress, or a new stage in the development of a person's life.

Milestones appear at predictable points throughout our journey from young adulthood until our senior years. School graduations, weddings, anniversaries and retirement are some of the more important and common ones that come to mind. Others, like job promotions or awards, are interspersed among them. These events are significant as well and offer an excellent opportunity to impart a blessing.

Young adulthood

Blessing is of such importance at this stage of life that the heavenly Father was not willing to permit Jesus to begin His adult ministry without it. Before Jesus preached even one sermon, or performed even one miracle, it was the Father's will that He receive a blessing given at the time of His adult baptismal ceremony. This blessing included a meaningful touch in the form of the dove and words of affirmation as the Father spoke directly to His Son saying: "You are my beloved Son, and I am fully pleased with you" (Mark 1:11 NLT).

This was definitely a milestone event, marking a new phase of Jesus' life. After that moment Jesus did not return to live at home with His parents; instead He was led by the Spirit to the desert for a final test before He launched His public ministry. He began this new phase with the unshakable assurance of His Father's favor.

The transition into our life's calling doesn't always happen as quickly or dramatically as it did for Jesus. However, between the ages of 20 and 30 most young adults face the likelihood of making several transitions in a few short years. These may include graduation from high school, moving away from their parents' home, developing a new set of friends, graduation from post secondary education and possibly marriage. And like Jesus, they too have moments when they still need to hear the voice of parental affirmation.

Our youngest son Mark is a runner. I made it a habit to attend most of his cross country races in high school in order to help him with strategy and to shout encouragement. At the qualifying race for the provincial championships, moments before the race began, he pointed at a forest in the distance and asked, "Dad will you please stand over there today?" I wondered if perhaps he was embarrassed to have an enthusiastic father so close to the action, but before I could comment Mark added, "You can't see it from here, Dad, but on the last lap in the forest is a very steep hill and that would be a great place to hear your voice."

After I swallowed the lump in my throat I gave him a light pat on the shoulder and assured him that he would indeed hear my voice at that crucial place. Thirty minutes later, after Mark had played a key role in qualifying his team for the finals, his coach came to me and asked, "What got into your son today? How did he pass so many runners on that last lap?"

We all run our best race when those we love position themselves in a place where they can offer genuine encouragement at the time when it is most needed!

There is no rule to say when to give that shout of encouragement. It depends upon the race your child is running and how they are responding to each new challenge. One couple I know decided that the right time to give a special blessing to their daughter was on the occasion of her first move out on her own. They planned a dinner event for the immediate family and her grandparents. Her mother describes it this way:

To give our young adult daughter a blessing, we chose the occasion of her moving into her own apartment to attend college. At the end of the meal, we spoke aloud what we had written for her. The blessing included affirmation of many things, including our pride in her for her godly characteristics and her special abilities and gifts. We made certain that she knew 'You have what it takes to make it!' Then we blessed many aspects of her future, including her marriage, family, work, and health. We included a Scripture verse at the end. Having printed it off with a border and graphics, we presented the blessing to her at the end of the meal as a keepsake and a reminder of God's love and ours.

Graduations

Parents must not abdicate their role of blessing to the professionals during this time of their child's life. This was made clear to me on the day our eldest son David graduated from high school. That afternoon Melissa and I sat in semi-darkness in the elaborately decorated gymnasium waiting for more than an hour for David to appear. The hundreds of graduates waited at the side of the platform for their turn at basking in 20 seconds of fame. One by one they crossed the stage while their grades, accomplishments and plans for the future were broadcast over the loudspeakers. The accolades accorded each student were restricted to grades, scholarships and choice of post secondary education. Eventually our son took his turn, received his diploma and took a seat in the crowd as his enrollment in an Honors Business program was announced.

It was over rather quickly, and I was left with a feeling of incompleteness about the event. Much more needed to be said about our son's character and future, and I could not expect professional educators to recognize or verbalize it. That was my job. Although Melissa and I later added our words of affirmation and a gift, I wished I had planned a more elaborate blessing ceremony to follow his graduation. Since then, we have taken every opportunity to bless him.

Adult baptisms

An obvious milestone occurs when a person is born again, or discovers a new-found faith in Jesus Christ. Some churches practice "believer baptisms" for these new Christians. When Melissa and I served as pastors, we intentionally added spoken blessings to new believers' baptism ceremonies. Family members were instructed how to craft a blessing and then wrote it out beforehand. Just before the candidate was baptized family members and/or friends came forward and read their pre-written blessings. This simple procedure profoundly touched the lives of everyone involved and never failed to make an impact on the listeners, including visiting family who had not yet found their own faith in Christ.

Weddings

When a child gets married, the Parental Blessing helps the new couple to "leave and cleave." This old English idiom refers to the young couple's need to leave their parents' homes and begin a new home together. The ceremony and reception represent unparalleled opportunities to communicate this crucial life blessing. There are unlimited varieties of symbolic acts, speeches and spoken blessings that can add a depth of meaning to the standard traditions. In recent years, when I perform weddings I encourage the bride and groom to request a parental blessing as part of the ceremony (see Wedding Ceremonies Part Two, Section B). As the couple enters into their new joint identity, they need room to grow. The parental role shifts from coach to consultant, the difference being that a consultant answers questions only when asked.

Birthdays

Birthdays are obvious milestones, tailor-made for the delivery of a blessing. Your birthday is the one day in each year when other people celebrate you! The traditional practice of giving cards and gifts opens the door for crafting a spoken blessing at any age. A happy birthday becomes a blessed birthday when we use words, deeds and ceremonies to communicate to the person the significance and value they have both in God's eyes and ours.

It is common to have surprise birthday parties to mark milestones such as 18, 21 or anything thereafter that ends in a zero. One year, in order to achieve complete surprise, Melissa planned a 48th birthday blessing party for me knowing I wasn't expecting anything for another two years. She selected a few couples who had shared in our ministry and invited them to a surprise dinner party. After dessert each couple read or spoke a prepared blessing. The depth of our relationships and the wisdom of their words provided a profound moment for me. I have kept those blessings and still read them from time to time.

Mid-life milestones

From promotions and new jobs, to birthdays, anniversaries and retirements, any transition in life can become an opportunity to give a blessing. For example, married couples often decide to renew their marriage vows at significant points such as their 25th or 30th wedding anniversaries. In addition to repeating marriage vows, couples may choose to prepare a spoken blessing to be read to their life partner. This is also an ideal time for friends, family and children to 'get in on the act" by preparing a blessing for the couple.

Senior years

Blessing cannot be separated from honor. One makes room for the other. When we honor someone, we make a decision to place them in a position of high value, worth and respect. As the milestones accumulate, it is increasingly important to demonstrate honor when giving a spoken blessing.

Upon their return to the U.S., a retiring missionary couple, who had served faithfully for 39 years, received only a fill-in-the-blank paper certificate as an acknowledgment of their decades of fruitful service. I was upset at the lack of honor that had been demonstrated by their mission board. When I was made aware of the situation, I arranged a blessing ceremony for the couple in the presence of many of the men and women they had mentored. God's presence filled the room as the blessing filled the missionaries' hearts.

Nowhere do honor and blessing have a stronger connection than in the relationship between parents and children. "honor your mother and father," is the only one of the ten commandments that ends with a promise: "You will live a long life, full of blessing" (Ephesians 6:2-3 NLT).

These Scriptures tell us clearly that the initiative for blessing during the senior years must shift from parents to children. The virtuous woman described in Proverbs 31 was honored by her children: "They arose and called her blessed." It's up to the younger generation to initiate the words, deeds and ceremonies that firmly establish honor and communicate worth and value in the lives of aging parents. The results can be wonderful.

At the 50th wedding anniversary of Melissa's parents, family from all over North America were invited. More than 40 came, including almost every member of the original wedding party. Special touches included skits, pictures and our daughter modeling her grandmother's wedding dress.

During the renewal-of-vows ceremony, we invited the honored couple to stand at the altar as they might have on their wedding day. They were surrounded by their six adult children who in turn were encircled by 18 grandchildren. Together, the adult children read a prepared blessing that began with the words, "Today we rise up and call you blessed." The blessing honored them for more than half a century of faithful marriage and service to their family and to the Lord.

The last milestone

The last milestone is the end of the journey; the marker is the gravestone. At most funeral services someone gives a eulogy which is, in one sense, a blessing for the departed loved one. In fact, the root word for blessing in Greek is *eulogeo,* which means to speak well of someone with praise. Unfortunately, while those who remain may be inspired by the words, they are of no value to the person being eulogized! Therefore before a loved one passes from this life to the next, a blessing ought to be spoken to them as well. God is glorified when we lay aside differences and past offenses and extend forgiveness in order to make room for blessing. Even if it seems difficult to bless the person at the time, it is much easier than living with life-long regret at having missed the opportunity. I suggest, *carpe diem* – seize the day! Tomorrow may not offer another chance.

Truth to go

Take time to pause and reflect. This chapter covered a wide range of years and circumstances.

- What milestones are loved ones in your life about to encounter? How might you plan to incorporate a blessing ceremony for them?
- Is there a senior adult in your life who has not been fully honored for their service to others? If so, how might you initiate and plan a blessing event for this person?
- Are your parents in their senior years? Consider holding a blessing event in their honor.

CHAPTER 9

What Single Parent Families Need

Most single parent families are led by women. Single moms learn to accept challenges that many two-parent families do not experience. They can always use a little help from their friends.[1]

Mothers are designed by God to bear and nurture children. A mother is her child's prime source of security and identity in the earliest years of life. Fathers are designed "call forth" children into their adult identities. During teen years they are to take the lead as a life coach. These complementary roles of parents can be pictured using the metaphor from Psalm 127:4: "Like arrows in the hands of a warrior are sons born in one's youth..."

Children arrive in the hands of parents like a stick that must be carefully shaped before it is eventually shot forth to reach its target. A mother focuses upon shaping the bow (the home environment), and the father focuses upon loading the arrow into the bow, aiming and releasing it toward the target (i.e. their future life outside the home).

A single mom who is diligent can do a wonderful job on her own to shape an excellent bow for her "little arrows," but who will help her fire them toward their target in life?

When children reach teen years without a father figure in sight, they need a blessing that is extremely difficult for a mother to give on her own. Women who are "spiritually single" – whose husbands do not share their faith commitment – often face this same dilemma.

When they are available, the extended families of single parents ought to rally around to help deliver the family blessing (see 1 Timothy 5:4). An email we received from the mother of a teenage boy provides an example of how well that can work:

The day of the blessing went extremely well. You had suggested that I ask each person who is close to Jamie to speak blessings in his life in each area outlined in the book. I did, and it was so great to have my parents, my sister and very good friends of the family all speak blessings into Jamie's life for the present and future. Jamie was so touched. He is too "cool" to cry, but I noticed his eyes were filling with tears at one point. It was so powerful to see God at work. We felt His presence without a doubt.

Since then so much has happened. God continues to work His miracles. My son has more self-confidence than he had before. His grades have improved. His relationships with peers are better and he has stepped up to a leadership role on his basketball team. He became captain of the team, and it has been amazing to see this shy boy blossom to the point where he is giving directions to his team mates. Even when he disagrees with the referees, he calmly speaks with them during the break. At times I cannot believe it is the same child. I notice that he is willing to take the initiative in reading the Bible, and he asks for prayer more often now when he has needs.

I have to say, it all started with the blessing party last September.

If no extended family members are available, then it's the duty of the family of God, the Church, to pick up the slack. Standing in the "blessing gap" for children who have no father figure can present a wonderful opportunity for people to experience the power of God.

A single mother with a son and younger daughter moved to our neighborhood from another country. She was looking for friendship and began to attend the church I pastored at the time. Shortly afterward the mom came to faith in Christ, but her 13-year-old son (whom I will call Steve) had little interest in her faith, or in God. During the next seven or eight years there were predictable periods of conflict between the mother and her son, and a few moments of outright rebellion. However, this mom never exhibited self-pity. She worked hard to support her family and integrated herself into the mainstream of church life. She served others and even went on a mission trip. She did everything she could, but she couldn't give her son a father's blessing.

During the period when her son was a teen, two or three men, myself included, decided to make ourselves available to mentor Steve. We found reasons to include him in social activities so that he would have a healthy model of extended family. Once I chartered a boat and took my own sons plus Steve on a fishing trip. When I told the owner of the boat what I was doing, he let Steve come for free!

Steve was in his early 20s by the time his mom had learned about giving a Family Blessing. She decided that it was not too late, so she threw a party for him on his birthday and included several adults who had played a significant role in Steve's development. (The fact that Steve's mother also needed blessing should not be overlooked. Counselors, pastors and friends from our church family helped her to work through her issues of forgiveness and missed blessings.)

Although I was away on a ministry trip on that date, I nevertheless carefully took the time to write out a Young Adult Blessing for Steve to be read at his party. I want to share a portion of that blessing as an example and inspiration for other men who may wish to bless a young man or woman in similar circumstances to Steve's:

Steve, although, I cannot be here in person to read this to you, that does not diminish the truth carried in these words.

As we all pause and reflect on your birthday about the man you have become and where God will take you, I want to say I am proud of you.

You had just entered teen years when we first met, and

I will never forget watching you wrestle with my eldest son Dave that day and thinking "I like this boy! He's fun!"

You and your mom weathered some difficult times during your teen years, but none of us ever doubted for a minute that you would one day find the inner strength to focus your life upon a worthy goal, and in so doing find purpose and fulfillment.

A certain night many years ago as you sat sullenly in the back row during a church service, you reluctantly permitted me to pray for you. As I laid my hand on your shoulder, you immediately felt the presence of God, and asked, "What do you have in your hand?"

I found it winsome that you were trying hard not to be a part of the service, but at the same time you were able to sense the presence of God! This was a sign of things to come in your life.

A few years later as you were becoming a man, you were also becoming a man of faith. Your spiritual journey has also impacted your fiancée and now she has found faith in Jesus Christ.

You also have a highly developed sense of righteousness which is reflected in your indignation at unfairness of any kind. As you enter your career, I know that you will combine your skill and passion for justice to truly become a man of influence for good.

I believe in you and I am truly excited to see where God will be taking you in the years ahead.

I bless you with open doors, that you will always be in the right place at the right time to take advantage of God's opportunities for your life.

I bless you with spiritual wisdom, that you will always live with a healthy sense of respect for the consequences of all your actions.

I bless your relationships, beginning with your family life and continuing to friendships and business relationships outside your home.

May you always have God's favor as you learn to walk

in obedience to the unique life calling that you have been prepared for all these years.

And remember, you do not journey alone. In addition to your family, friends and mentors, I will make myself available to you as often as I can when you need advice or prayer. I consider you a life-long friend and am happy to offer counsel in any circumstance."

Since then Steve moved to another city, graduated from university, and is now married with two children. He still calls or visits several times a year, especially when he needs counsel or advice. He openly states that the love of his mom and the influence of two or three male mentors is responsible for the success he enjoys today in his family. That's the kind of help that single parents and their children need.

Truth to go
To bless a single parent and their children:
- The opportunity to give a spoken blessing flows from a life commitment. Count the cost before you begin. You do not want to raise expectations that you cannot fulfill. Be prayerful in your choice of single parent families alongside whom you will walk.
- Set boundaries and verbalize the extent of your commitment. Begin slowly so that you don't create unrealistic expectations in your prospect.
- Invite a single parent family to join you in some of your family events.

For single parents:
You may not be able to change your marital status, but you can compensate for the lack of a second parent's blessing in your home:
- Be open to your own need for spiritual and emotional health. Make it a priority to recover your own missed blessings, and learn to be a good forgiver.
- Find a church that welcomes single parents and their

children. Do your best to integrate into church life activities.

- Get to know those in your church with a heart for single parents. These folk are the most likely to become available to assist you in blessing your teens.
- For single moms: if there is no father figure in your children's lives, then craft the kind of blessing you wish a father would give, and speak it to them yourself. Regardless of who delivers the blessings during teen years, our heavenly Father can accomplish His work in the lives of your children.

[1] I know that there are also some faithful single parent dads out there, however this chapter will focus primarily upon the many moms whose children often lack a healthy father influence.

CHAPTER 10

Blessing a Person's Name

Nothing is more personal than a name. It was the first gift your parents gave you. It will last your entire lifetime.

There is an inherent authority in the assigning of a name. God gave Adam authority to rule over the Earth. Adam exercised that authority by fulfilling his God-given assignment of naming all the animals (see Genesis 2:20).

Parents exercise the authority God gave Adam by naming their children. Naming is part of the stewardship of parenting, and because it is a great responsibility, parents should choose names for their children prayerfully and carefully.

In biblical times, names were chosen to reflect identity as well as to prophesy destiny. A person was given a name that was connected to their nature. For example, "Abraham" means father of a multitude.

The blessing imparted by the name was so important to God that John the Baptist's father Zechariah was struck dumb until he wrote on a tablet, "His name is John." He then made a prophetic announcement about John's identity and destiny (see Luke 1:57-66).

The ancient Hebrews demonstrated an understanding of the power of names to shape destiny.

In a period of time when Israel was largely backslidden, a couple from the region of Tishbe boldly decided to name their child Elijah, meaning God is Great. We know nothing else about Elijah's parents except that they must have had great faith to name their child, God is Great, during a very low point in Israel's history. Whenever his parents addressed him, he heard them say, God is Great! Can you imagine what that sounded like when he was a toddler?

God is Great – eat your breakfast!
God is Great – put your clothes away!
God is Great – play nicely with your friends!

No wonder Elijah had no problem facing down 450 prophets of Baal on Mount Carmel (see 1 Kings 18:20). When he had to prove that the God of Israel was great, and immeasurably more powerful than Baal, he likely shrugged and thought to himself, No problem – God is Great! Then he turned to those present and said, Pour more water on that altar and watch this....

Traditionally our North American culture has not placed such an emphasis upon the meaning of names, yet many parents are now discovering the value of prayerfully selecting the names of their newborn children. My wife Melissa and I have always believed in the significance of names. We sought God's guidance when choosing the name for each of our three children. Today, more than 20 years later, it is remarkable to observe how well our children's names fit their individual characters.

Discovering the meaning of a name

What happens when a name is chosen without specific forethought given to the relationship between the name and the child's identity? Even in such cases, I am surprised to discover how often God's hand seems to have been working in advance to ensure that a person's name becomes a blessing upon the person's identity. A remarkable example came from a friend who forwarded the following e-mail after reading our teaching on the importance of names:

I hadn't thought of it before, but the story of our daughter's name has a spiritual meaning as a Name Blessing.
My husband's name is Ken and I'm Daina. Before our daughter was born I was playing with combinations

of our names to make a name for our daughter (I had made up my mind she would be a girl!) I came up with the name, Kenda (KEN and DAina). When she was born, we named her Kenda. Not long after, I was flipping through a baby name book when, to my surprise, I found the name Kenda. I learned that it is an American Indian name meaning, "child of the Living Waters"! Talk about God putting destiny in a name!

A Name Blessing does not always present itself so clearly or quickly as it did for Ken and Daina.

Research is often required to uncover a meaning that may have been previously unnoticed. Sometimes the research will produce variations of meaning. In these situations, it is necessary to trust the leading of the Holy Spirit as you prayerfully choose the most relevant meaning.

Once in a while it may be difficult to find the meaning of a uniquely crafted or unusual name. In this case I usually find a name that is closest to the sound of the person's actual name.

Another option may be to go beyond given names to research the surname (family name).

Redeeming the meaning of a name

When you are confronted with a name that does not appear to have a positive meaning, be prepared to do a little "detective" work to find the God story in the name! For example a woman named Wendy, which means 'wanderer', took hold of a new sense of purpose for her name when she was used of God to help those who wander from their faith to return to the Lord.

Another way to bless a name that lacks a positive meaning is to draw upon the character qualities of other people with the same name. A classic example where this is helpful is the name Mary, which comes from the Hebrew word mara, meaning bitter. It doesn't sound like much of a blessing. However, throughout history many godly women have been named Mary and can be used as positive namesakes, including Mary, Jesus' earthly mother.

Truth to go

Here's how to give a Name Blessing:

- **Pray** – ask the Lord to reveal His purpose and meaning in the person's name.
- **Research** – look in different sources such as *The Name Book* by Dorothy Astoria. The internet has a plethora of websites that give meanings for names. Research the history of the family name, if desired.
- **Interview** the person to discover a possible "God story" connected to the manner in which they received their name.
- **Select a Scripture** that is compatible with the meaning of the name once you have discovered that meaning. Write a Scriptural connotation in one sentence that links the name with a biblical truth.
- **Prepare a card or plaque** that summarizes the information you have gleaned.
- **Perform a small Name Blessing ceremony** that includes presenting the person with their card or plaque.
- **Conclude the ceremony with a prayer** to "set the seal" of God's love upon their heart through the meaning of their name.

CHAPTER 11

When Blessing Doesn't Make Sense

Someone once said, "Life is something that happens while you are planning something else."

On occasion, the "something that happens" is so troubling that trying to give a blessing doesn't seem to make sense.

This would prove to be tragically true for friends of ours whom I will call Bill and Sandra. They have two children – a son and a daughter – what some call a "millionaire's family." However they felt like anything but millionaires the day the phone call came that their son Carl had overdosed on drugs leading to severe brain damage. When her son survived against the doctor's expectations, Sandra knew immediately that God had a plan and she prayed that He would somehow be glorified through the difficult days that were certain to follow. Here's the inspiring story in her own words:

Carl had been a relatively easy child to raise, making a commitment to Christ early and re-affirming that commitment as a teen. But as a young man in his 20s he just did not seem able to find his place in this world. He became angry, shut us out of his life to a large degree, and things just started spiraling downward, until at age 27 when he made an attempt on his life with an overdose of Tylenol. As a result, he required a liver transplant and had a complication of a brain injury.

During the initial days after the incident, the question, Why? never really entered my mind. I knew beyond [doubt] that God is good, no matter what the circumstances in our life. I knew that God intended to use this situation for Carl's good.

After lots of testing we received a prognosis for Carl from his neurologist. He told us that ... Carl would not walk, talk, eat or breathe on his own; that if he could see, he would not be able to interpret what he saw; and that he would never recognize us or be able to live outside an institution.

I believe the neurologist interpreted the data correctly, but God intervened. Not one of those limitations is a reality today.

Carl's life before this event had been painful for us all, and I was more than ready to let him go. But as soon as the doctor gave us his prognosis, I said, "I cannot accept that." I asked the nurses not to repeat what was said to anyone who might visit.

Our pastor came to the hospital and prayed a "prayer of agreement" with us to receive God's plan for Carl. The progress Carl made was miraculous. He began walking, talking, and breathing on his own. He became able to eat anything he wanted. Contrary to the prognosis, he does know us, and just about anyone else he knew before.

I had written a blessing for Carl a couple of years before, but he was not open to receiving anything like that from us. Two months into his recovery it was his birthday, and I felt this was the right time to bless him. He was still unable at this point really to receive what we were saying on an intellectual level, but I knew that his spirit was available to receive it. Even though I could not see a response in Carl's face as we blessed him, I had peace that this was the right time, and any benefit he was to receive from his blessing would not be inhibited by his condition.

The blessing

Carl you have been through a lot in your life, but you have endured by the strength that God has placed in you. He has preserved you.

Carl you are the son of His dreams, some men dream of having a son who is a football star or a surgeon, but God dreamt of you. You are His dream, His creation. Carl you give others grace and forgiveness, and there is grace and forgiveness for you.

God has preserved you for a reason – to fulfill the plans He has for you.

We call you to step out into the plans your Father has for you. You are worthy. You qualify for the good things He holds in store for you.

Carl you are a man of strength, gentleness, endurance, courage, and honor.

We break the power of every word spoken against you and your future, in Jesus name.

We bless every aspect of your life.

May God's favor be on you as you deal with family, peers, authorities, co-workers, and acquaintances, that they would see you as your heavenly Father does; that their eyes would be opened to all the good things He has placed inside you.

We bless your health and recovery, that you would walk in the physical, emotional, and spiritual wholeness that Christ died to give you.

We bless your future marriage, that you would find a partner who can be blessed by your strengths and who can be a blessing to you.

We bless your ability to earn a living, that not only you would earn enough money, but that money would provide you and your family with a home and all that is necessary for a secure life.

We bless your possessions, that they would serve you and not be a drain on your finances.

We bless your spiritual life, that you would enjoy intimacy with your Creator, and that His every plan for you would be fulfilled.

The results
Within a week Carl ... recognize[d] me as his mom,

*and invited Christ into his life. God has been so good
to us this past year. His provision has been miraculous
and generous; His timing perfect in every detail. And
His favor has been obvious in our dealings with the
medical community, and government bureaucracy.
Does he still have a long way to go? Sure, but he has
come so far already, I am not even asking what will be
the final outcome. I just know that everything is working... according to God's plan, and I have peace. I am
so enjoying my son.*

Bill and Sandra believe that Carl's change in behavior
and openness to the Lord were a direct result. Carl has said
to his parents "I'm a new man!" He understands that
something good has happened, and spiritually his heart is
more open now than it ever was before he entered the hospital.

We rarely get to choose the price we have to pay for what
we want the most. When parents want a blessed child who
loves God, they have no way of knowing what route that
child may have to take to get there.

I am very impressed with the love Carl's parents exhibited and their acceptance of the new reality
unceremoniously thrust upon them. No victim mentality
there! Sandra refused to become tangled in the classic question, Why me? She learned a crucial lesson for all those
who suffer – that the question, Why? may never be
answered in this life. Bill and Sandra focused upon what
they could do, rather than asking why this happened to
them, and demonstrated a willingness to cooperate with
God at any turn of events.

Carl may never become married, read a book, or live on
his own again, but he knows that he is a "new man" and
that he is loved by his parents and by his Saviour. One day
he will trade his damaged mind for a brand new flawless
model. Then Carl will have eternity to thank God for parents who understood and applied the principles of blessing
in spite of the obstacles placed in their path.

It's impossible to address every situation that you and others may face in life. Bill and Sandra's story is but one example of the huge hurdles that can be strewn across the path that we must walk in life. No matter what you may encounter, the Holy Spirit can reveal the heavenly Father's plan and give you understanding of how to bring a blessing into your difficult circumstances.

Truth to go

If you have encountered difficulty or suffering that causes you to question God's purpose or plan, then perhaps you may want to begin the search for blessing with this prayer:

Dear heavenly Father: I don't understand why this situation has occurred and I know I cannot handle it in my own strength. I know that your Word in Romans 8:28 says you cause all things to work together for good to those who love God. So I thank you for the plan you have already devised to help me through this time. I ask for you to reveal to me how you can be glorified through this circumstance. I ask that you give me your strength to walk it through. And I ask that you grant me understanding how to receive and give blessing to everyone who is involved. I ask these things believing that you want to answer each request. In Jesus Name, Amen.

CHAPTER 12

Frequently Asked Questions

This chapter is comprised of some of the most frequently asked questions we receive and the answers we most frequently give to these questions. If you don't find *your* question answered in this chapter, then contact us through our website and we will do our best to respond.

Q. Can I give a blessing when I haven't yet received family blessings myself?

Yes... sometimes. Any work the Holy Spirit performs through us is always by GRACE. Therefore we can expect that the Holy Spirit will be actively partnering with us when we give a spoken blessing. At times God's Spirit will speak directly to the person as we bless them, and will create an impact that goes beyond our words and actions. However, there are two ways in which the lack of blessing can impair your ability to bless others.

The first has to do with forgiveness. When unforgiveness remains in your heart, the effect of a spoken blessing is weakened. The words of Jesus in the Gospels lead us to understand that the flow of the Holy Spirit through your life is directly proportional to the measure of forgiveness you extend to others (see Mark 11:25). Experiencing the grace of forgiveness will "un-kink the hose" and permit blessing to flow through your life.

The second is this: where the truth is absent, the enemy will always fill the void with a lie. For example, people who have had to strive for their parents' blessing may believe that children need to earn the blessing of a parent. They in turn will have difficulty releasing an unconditional blessing upon their own children.

There is no doubt that as you continue to recover your own missed blessings, your ability to bless others will be strengthened!

Q. I wish I had learned the value of blessing sooner in life. Is it too late to start blessing my children when they are all grown adults?

Someone has said, "The best time to plant a tree is 25 years ago and the second best time is today." Although we cannot recover the time that is lost, it's NEVER too late to start blessing! A good place to begin is to review your relationship with your children in light of the seven stages of blessing and the major life questions. Determine which of these questions remain unanswered in your children's lives. You can still deliver a spoken blessing many years after the fact with very powerful results. Plan to include a blessing ceremony in a family event. You can begin the blessing by saying "I am sorry that I did not understand the power of blessing when you were younger. However today I do understand and therefore I want to bless you with these words..." Before you plan such an event, it is advisable to determine if there are any outstanding relationship issues that need to be addressed before the blessing will be welcomed.

Q. Can I bless someone who is indifferent or resistant to my blessing?

Just as it is difficult to give something you have not received, it is also very difficult to give something to someone who is not ready to receive it. In Revelation 3:20 Jesus says, "Here I am! I stand at the door and knock. If anyone hears my voice and opens the door, I will come in ..."

The same "if" applies to delivering a blessing – it cannot be imposed upon anyone. Sometimes all that is required is an explanation of the purpose and the value of the blessing to be given. However, when a person remains indifferent or resistant, the path to take requires prayer for wisdom and patience.

Parents of teenage or adult children often encounter the

need to "untangle" past relationship issues before a parental blessing can be effective. It is helpful to ask the Holy Spirit to reveal what has been blocking the path of blessing. Is there a forgiveness issue, an unresolved offense or misunderstanding?

Sometimes when relationships are strained, delivering a written blessing is preferable, as it permits the recipient to consider the truth without a face to face encounter.

Q. Are parents able to fully bless their adopted children?

Adopted children face two additional major life questions: What is my biological identity? And, Why was I given away? Adoptive parents need to be ready to lovingly engage their children in the process of answering these crucial questions. The truth that an adopted child needs to understand in order to live a fully blessed life is summarized by this statement: Whatever the circumstances were that led to the adoption, God's best plan for my life will be fulfilled by bringing me into the adoptive family.

Q. Are blessings only for professing Christians?

a) Can I give a blessing to someone who doesn't share my faith perspective?

Anyone can receive a blessing if they have an open heart and mind. Always ask for permission before giving a blessing to anyone, regardless of their faith perspective. If God has given you insight into a person's character or future, then a blessing can be powerfully effective regardless of that person's faith perspective. In fact a blessing often softens the heart of a non-believing person so that they are more receptive to God's love. Blessing involves intimacy, and some people may be uncomfortable with being forced to be part of a blessing ceremony. Use discretion and ask for God's wisdom and discernment.

b) Can a person who is not a professing Christian give a blessing?

Yes, if the conditions apply regarding relationships and permission (see previous questions). For example, at a wedding I conducted, the parents of the groom were not church goers, nor did they profess any particular faith. However, having heard that the bride's mother was giving a blessing, the groom's mother decided that she wanted to bless her son and his new bride on their wedding day. Not really knowing what to do, she looked up "blessing" on the internet in order to get some guidance. She ended up speaking a beautiful blessing to the couple at the reception. Afterward she told us, "I have never felt anything so powerful in my life. I cannot put words to my emotion or the source of them. I was standing there speaking, and although I knew that I had written the words, as I spoke them it seemed as if they were not coming from me." She was feeling the presence of God who was partnering with her blessing at that moment!

Q. Should I give a blessing even if I don't agree with choices being made in the person's life?

Parents can place their relationship with a child at risk when important blessings are withheld as a means of showing disapproval. If in the parent's judgment a child is making an obviously bad decision, then it may be wise to withhold the blessing temporarily while making every reasonable attempt to resolve the issue. If an agreement cannot be reached, a parent can bless their child without endorsing the child's decisions.

An example of this is contained in an e-mail I received from a missionary couple who now serve as directors of an orphanage in Africa. The wife writes:

This testimony is (from) a memory I had of my marriage. I was not serving God at that point in my life, nor did I have any intention of doing so again, and I was to be engaged to the man who would become my wonderful husband. My dad had pulled me aside and asked me to pray about the engagement sincerely.

However as God and I weren't talking at that point, our engagement went forward.

As a Christian now, I cry every time I remember the pain I caused my dad and mom, when they realized they would lose me because I was prepared to walk away from family if they stood opposed to my wedding. And I remember as if it was yesterday, my dad saying "I can see I'm going to lose you otherwise, so I give you my blessing." He repeated it when we went inside and announced to my mom that we were engaged.

After reading your book I realize that my dad's blessing may have been the reason God has so blessed our marriage, and why girlfriends who have made similar decisions (without their parent's blessing) have instead experienced heartache and marriage breakups. I believe the power of my family's prayers after that blessing, is why seven years ago, my husband and I gave our lives to Jesus Christ. He grew us into leadership and now overseas to affect the lives of children in Africa. Thank you for your teaching and guidance.

Q. Does blessing solve every emotional issue?

No it does not. There are different sources for emotional problems. Some persons have chemical imbalances which produce mood disorders. A spoken blessing cannot be expected to cure this condition. Persons suffering from long-standing addictions or psychological problems may also require professional help in addition to a spoken blessing before they acquire the ability to change. For more information on this subject, we recommend resources by Dr. Grant Mullen (see Additional Media Resources, page 106).

Q. What if the person I want to bless does not live close to me?

If you live far away from the person you wish to bless, or if you are just not comfortable giving a spoken message, a blessing in writing can be very powerful and can carry the same words of honor and value that a spoken blessing can bring. Using the instructions in Chapter 4, prayerfully craft the blessing the same way you would as if you were speaking face to face. In the place of a meaningful touch, you may want to include a memento such as a meaningful photo. Ask for God's presence to accompany the words as you mail or e-mail it. Perhaps a trusted friend or family member can review the words of the blessing before you send them.

Q. Can I bless my parents if they have not yet blessed me?

I believe that every family line has a generational blessing to give and receive. As adult children "rise up" and call their parents blessed, there is much more opportunity for the blessing to be revealed and, of course, to be passed to the following generations (see Proverbs 31:28).

Adults who have yet to receive their parents' blessing can bless them providing the parents are willing to receive that blessing. The same issues arise as covered in the first question in this chapter. In other words, you must first be willing to forgive and to do the necessary work to recover your own missed blessings. Chapter 14 in *The Power of Blessing* book gives an inspiring example of a couple who decided, after they recovered their own missed blessings, to make a commitment to bless the husband's parents at every opportunity, such as family gatherings and personal visits. Eventually this resulted in a reconciliation and mutual blessing that was passed along to the grandchildren. (This couple is also featured on DVD #10 of *The Power of Blessing* series.)

PART TWO
Tools of the Trade

SECTION A

Blessings for
Every Age & Stage

Family Tree Chart

Blessing Form

Major Life Questions

Blessings for the 7 Life Stages

Permission to Use the Blessings, Charts and Prayers

The blessings, charts and prayers in PART TWO of The Blessing Handbook include a mixture of items we have collected and those we have written ourselves. It is our desire that you use them to design personalized blessings for the people you love. However, some restrictions do apply for the reproduction of the blessings, charts or prayers for reasons other than your personal and private use.

1. Permission is granted to reproduce the blessings, charts and prayers in Part Two and/or to modify them for your own personal and private use without citing their source.

2. Permission is granted to reproduce the blessings, charts and prayers
   a) on electronic media for personal use or public presentations
   b) in print up to a maximum of 500 words provided that the source is cited in the format below:

   from *The Blessing Handbook*
   www.powerofblessing.com
   © 2007 Terry & Melissa Bone, used with permission

3. Permission to reprint more than 500 words from the blessings, charts and prayers for reasons other than your personal and private use must be requested in writing to:

   info@powerofblessing.com

Applicable fees will apply and may vary depending upon the nature of the request and the amount of material to be reprinted.

4. Requests to reprint other portions of *The Blessing Handbook* should also be made in writing to:

   info@powerofblessing.com

Family Tree/Generational Chart

enter information below each name on the chart

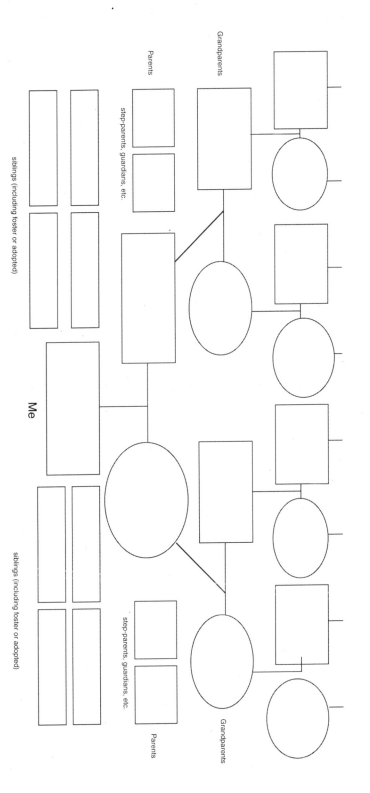

Grandparents

Parents

step-parents, guardians, etc.

siblings (including foster or adopted)

Father's side to the left

Me

Mother's side to the right

siblings (including foster or adopted)

step-parents, guardians, etc.

Parents

Grandparents

Prayerfully choose someone whom you can bless this week:

Name _____

Connect
Delivering the blessing in person is ideal. However, sending a written version to the person can also provide a meaningful connection.

How and when I plan to deliver this blessing:

_____

_____

_____

_____

Communicate
Record here what you intend to say – see "How to Craft a Blessing for Someone You Know"

A scripture verse:

_____

_____

_____

_____

_____

My Blessing:

_____

_____

_____

_____

_____

_____

_____

_____

_____

Communicate ...continued

_____

_____

_____

_____

_____

_____

_____

_____

_____

_____

_____

_____

_____

_____

_____

_____

_____

_____

_____

_____

Commit

If appropriate, indicate how you intend to help this person achieve
the desired future you have pictured for them

_____

_____

_____

_____

Major Life Questions

How do we know if we have been sufficiently blessed? We have developed a series of questions that correspond to each transitional stage of life. These questions help us determine the divine deposit of blessing we need in our soul in order to mature into our rightful identity and destiny. Once we have a truthful answer to these questions, we prosper in life without striving. When they remain unanswered, we struggle in life in spite of our valiant efforts.

Life Stages and their associated Major Life Questions

1. Conception	*Am I welcome in this world?*
2. Pregnancy	*Is there a safe place for me in the world?*
3. Birth	*Will my needs be met in this world?*
4. Early Childhood	*Who can I trust in this world?*
5. Teen Years	*Do I have what it takes to make it in this world?*
6. Adulthood	*What am I called to do in this world?*
	Who will share my journey?
7. Senior Years	*Am I still needed in this world?*

In the following pages of this section, we have listed 'generic' blessings suitable for each stage of life. These are designed to be a 'starting point' from which you can build a uniquely special blessing for someone you love.

Your 'Earth Day' – Life begins at conception!

We bless the day of your conception. Welcome to this world!

We bless your uniqueness. You are God's choice. Out of the hundreds of millions of possible combinations from your parents DNA, God determined that you would be you.

We bless the timing of your arrival on earth. You were no accident. God wanted you here for this time and for His purpose and so He gave permission for your spirit to be made alive on earth at exactly the right time regardless of the human circumstances.

We bless the destiny that was pre-planned for your life. Before the foundation of the earth, you existed in the mind and heart of God. All the days of your life were ordained before one of them came to be (see Psalm 139:16). May you discover the sheer joy of walking in the steps that God has ordered for your life.

We bless your eternal home. The same Heavenly Father who sent your spirit to earth is waiting to welcome you back to Himself one day. May your stay on earth include a rich personal relationship with Jesus Christ while He prepares a place in heaven just for you (see John 14:2).

Your Pre-born Days

We bless your pre-born days, when you were uniquely crafted and specifically designed for God's purpose.

We bless the formation of your body, that God performed in secret while you waited to be released to this world (see Psalm 139:13-15).

We bless your emotional life, that you may understand deep in your heart that God will always provide a safe place for you, a place of refuge on this earth from the forces that set themselves against you. May God's perfect love displace any fears in your life.

The Day of Your Birth

We bless the day of your birth. May your know that your needs will always be met according to the supply of the One who sent you to this earth to accomplish His purpose through you.

We bless your gender, for you were created to be a man/woman, according to God's design.

We bless your birth order, in the family to which you were given. May the timing of your arrival and the relationships with family members be used by God to perfect you according to His will.

We bless your mental growth, as you begin to process the world around you. May your ear gates and eye gates be guarded by those who care for you and keep you in their home.

We bless your spiritual journey. May it begin with a dedication to a faith community that follows Jesus Christ. May you be guarded and guided by human and angelic beings until you are old enough to make your own choices.

Your Early Childhood

We bless your early childhood, that you may learn to trust everyone who exercises godly authority in your life.

We bless your play times, that your mind may learn and grow to your full potential. May you be kept safe at all times.

We bless your mental development, that nothing would hinder the growth of your mind to its full potential.

We bless the development of your will, that you may be shaped in wisdom and love by those in authority in your life. May you learn to make wise choices in every life decision.

We bless your spiritual life, that you would understand and experience what it means to walk with God at a young age.

We bless your family relationships, that you would discover and enjoy a sense of belonging in a family that loves you. May you be kept safe from accidental emotional injury and improper discipline.

We bless your school experiences. May school be a safe place for you to learn and grow. May school authorities recognize and encourage your gifts and talents.

We bless your friendships. May you may be guided to make wise choices in every relationship outside your family circle.

Your Teen Years

We bless your teen years. You have what it takes to fulfill everything God has called you to do. As you apprentice for adulthood, may your unique talents and gifts be recognized and stimulated in preparation for your life's work.

We bless your physical development, that you would be content and happy in the body God has given you as it reaches maturity. May you enjoy excellent health.

We bless your mental development, that you will receive the necessary education and intellectual preparation for your life's work. May you appreciate both the process and outcome of learning.

We bless you spiritually, that you may have personal encounters with living God. May you experience consistent growth in your faith, day by day. May you be given the strength to resist temptation. May you learn to hear the voice of God's Spirit. May you develop a 'devotional habit' of prayer and Bible reading that lasts a lifetime.

We bless you socially, that you may experience true friendships, a good reputation, and a safe environment in which you feel loved and accepted for who you are.

We bless your life preparation. May these years truly serve as an apprenticeship period for adulthood. May you always be mentored in character and in your life's calling.

We bless your need to grow. May you learn from your mistakes and experiment with your gifts and talents. May you never fear to accept new challenges and test the limits of your capabilities within the boundaries set by godly authority.

Your Adult Identity

We bless your adult identity and your destiny in this world. May you discover the purpose for which God sent you to this earth and 'rule' in your God given area of authority.

May you learn God's ways and discern God's paths as you fulfill God's purpose for your life.

May you always follow the leading of God's Spirit in every decision you face.

May you never stop growing in the understanding and application of God's Word for your life.

We bless your marriage, that what God has joined together, no one would ever separate. May your life mate be your closest friend and most understanding companion. May you walk together in unity spiritually as well as emotionally.

We bless your children, that the generational blessing upon your family line would be passed on to them. May each child provide breadth and depth to your own life experience. May each one share your values in life and experience a personal walk with God.

We bless your relationships, that God would lead you to those who can mentor you as well as those who need to receive from what you have been given. May you never be without meaningful friendships.

We bless your finances, that you may always enjoy God's provision. We bless the work of your hands, that your industry and labor will bring abundance to provide for your family and to sow into others lives. May you always discern and obey the requirements for financial blessing. May you live securely without need or fear of want. May you learn to be content within the limits of God's provision.

We bless your health, that you may physically prosper and not succumb to sickness. May you prosper physically even as your soul prospers.

We bless your Christian witness, that you would carry with you the fragrance of Christ in all that you do. May your character and lifestyle be a witness to the truth of the God's promises. May you have many opportunities to share your personal faith and bear much fruit as you continue to abide in the vine, Jesus.

We bless you to go and bless others! May you give from the overflow of having received more than you can contain.

Your Senior Years

We bless your senior years, that you may continue to find a place of significance and purpose in this world. May you discover that you are needed and wanted by those of us who follow after you.

We bless your life's work. May you receive appropriate honor for your years of labor. May your contribution to the Kingdom of God on this earth be recognized and blessed.

We bless your life transition from working in the field to sitting in the gates. May you be sought out for wisdom and counsel so that your hard earned insights will benefit many in the years and generations to come.

We bless your health, that your strength will match the length of your days. May you be kept from accident, injury and illness.

Tools of the Trade

SECTION B

Sample Blessings, Ceremonies & Special Occasions

Pregnancy

Child Dedication

Teen Blessing

School Graduation Blessing

Wedding Blessings

25th Wedding Anniversary

Retirement & Seniors

House Blessing

We encourage you to modify the blessings found
in this section to suit your unique situation

Pregnancy Blessing
by Melissa Bone

For Mom: I (or we) bless this pregnancy. You are the right mom for this child... this baby is in the right body. I bless your body as you grow this little one inside. May the Lord 'strengthen your frame' (Is. 58:11) and give you a strong back to carry this child to full term. ! God has ordained for you to be its mother and you will be a good one. You have what it takes to raise this child, with God's help. He has overshadowed you, and what is conceived in you has been accomplished by the will of God and the help of the Holy Spirit.

May your baby come into the light in the fullness of time, not too late or too early! I bless your labor and delivery, that it would be smooth and free of complications. I bless you with good health, strength and peace - no fear of the future.

I call you blessed among women! Blessed is the fruit of your womb, blessed is this child you are bearing. And blessed is she who has believed that what the Lord has said to her will be accomplished! (see Luke 1:42-45)

For Baby: I bless you baby. Welcome to this world. You are in the right body, and you are right on time. You were supposed to be born at this time in history, and to these parents (or this mother if a single mom). I call you a blessed child. You are the right gender. I bless your development, the organs and systems that are in place now. God is putting the finishing touches on you now... *(depending on where the mother is in her gestation, I will often 'bless' what I know to be going on at her the stage in her trimester)* I bless you to 'stay put' until the fullness of time. I bless you to not come too early or too late, but right on time. I call your birthday a blessed day, when you come from the darkness into the light. I bless you in Jesus' name!

Child Dedication

There is no one like you on the face of the earth. **I bless your gender.** May you be glad that God has decided that you are to be a boy/girl.

I bless your mind to understand the plans God has for you.

I bless your heart to know that you are God's unique gift to the world.

I bless your ears to hear the voice of the God's Spirit.

I bless your eyes to see your world the way God sees it.

I bless your mouth to give praise to God and blessing to people.

I bless your feet to walk in the paths chosen for you by your Heavenly Father.

I bless your natural talents and your spiritual gifts. May you discover and develop them at an early age.

May everyone who looks after you in your childhood be kind and loving.

May your heart and mind be protected harsh words and lies.

May you love God with all you heart, mind and strength.

May you always choose your friends wisely.

May you discover God's first choice for a life partner.

May you find and fulfill your life's calling.

May you have God's provision and be kept in good health at every age and stage of your life.

The actual Blessing is followed by the prayer of Dedication which also invokes God's blessing upon the child...

Blessing for a New Teen based upon Luke 2:52

(Read Luke 2:52 aloud). Jesus had God's favor and therefore he matured in four ways as he entered teen years–mentally, socially, physically and spiritually.

Over these seven years, you will leave behind childhood and become an adult. Even now your new identity is emerging. I bless you to receive God's favor in the following ways:

I bless the development of your mind... For the first 12 years of your life, your brain has been growing – one trillion cells have been added since your life began. The growth of your brain is now complete, but not the growth of your mind! May you increase in knowledge and in wisdom. May you come to know your gifts and talents and learn to how to use them for good. May lies be recognized and rejected and truth be recognized and received.

I bless your physical development... May you grow strong and always be in good health.

May you be happy with the physical attributes God has given you and use your strength to serve Him.

I bless your social development... May you receive appropriate recognition for your emerging identity from your parents as well as teachers and other authority figures

May you continue to submit to godly authority figures.

May you have the strength to say NO to negative peer pressure.

May you always have meaningful & healthy friendships during teen years; may some of these friendships last a lifetime!

I bless your spiritual development... May you develop real wisdom, by listening to the advice of your parents, and always thinking about the consequences of your actions

May you have spiritual experiences that will positively impact you for the rest of your life

May you have a love for the Word of God and a growing knowledge of how it applies to your life (read Psalm 19:9-11).

Blessing for a School Graduation
(teenager or young adult)

The following basic format can be personalized and expanded.

Today, we celebrate the milestone in your life of
_____. Good work. We are proud of you and proud of
your accomplishment. This chapter in your life story is now
complete. From this day forward you enter a new phase in the
preparation of finding and fulfilling God's call upon your life.

We bless your mind. May you retain what you have
learned. May you have the understanding to be able to apply
the knowledge you have acquired in many life situations.

We bless your career. May your career be more than a
means to earn a living.

May it be a calling which becomes a means to serve others for the sake of God's kingdom on earth.

May God reveal to you the precise career path that is
planned for your life.

May you find joy and fulfillment in whatever work that
you do for the rest of your life.

We bless your character. Your educational degrees are
not your ultimate accomplishments in life.

The success of your career depends as much upon your
character as your education or training. What you know
may get you your first job, but who you are will determine
how far you progress.

Therefore as much as we celebrate your educational
achievement, we also bless these character qualities we see
in you _____.

We bless your future growth. May you never stop learning.

May you go beyond the accumulation of knowledge

May you be a life long learner who never stops growing
in wisdom and revelation.

(quote Ephesians 1:17)

We commit ourselves to always be available to assist you
in the follow ways _____.

Wedding Blessing

This blessing was written by Terry & Melissa Bone on the occasion of their daughter's marriage. It was included as part of the actual wedding ceremony. Before the couple said their own vows, the officiating minister took one minute to explain the purpose and the meaning of a blessing and then invited the parents of both the bride and the groom to come forward and stand beside their child – with one hand extended (or gently touching) the child's shoulder. As the minister read the blessing phrase by phrase, the parents repeated it aloud in unison phrase by phrase. It was followed by 'hugs and kisses all around' (with parents being very careful not to ruffle the bride's make-up or dress!)

We call this day a blessed day for all of us.

We recognize the eternal plan of God in bringing each of us to this momentous occasion

We acknowledge that it is God's grace that has prepared you for this day from birth.

We bless your choice of life partner and we believe that you are God's first choice for each other.

We release you from our home with our blessing.

We bless the establishing of your own home together.

We commit ourselves to be available for counsel and assistance whenever you call upon us.

We commit ourselves to pray for you often trusting the Holy Spirit to prompt us.

May God guide your every step so that you may fulfill His highest purpose for your lives.

May God provide for your every need at every stage of your journey together.

May you be blessed with children of your own in God's perfect timing.

May the same blessing that you have received today be passed on to your children and grandchildren.

A Blessing for a Son & Daughter-in-law
On their wedding day

To our Son:

We bless you today on this your wedding day. Since the day we knew of your conception we have loved and cherished you. You have always been loved, wanted and welcome in our lives and in our hearts. The Lord blessed us with you, a wonderful son.

We bless you today as a bridegroom and rejoice with you in the celebration of your love and commitment to _____, your wife. We bless you as a husband to take leadership and be the spiritual head of your family.

Our prayers for you since you were little is that you would become a "mighty man of God".

May the Lord bless you with wisdom and discernment so that you may become a good and loving husband.

May the Lord bless you with faithfulness, strength and a love that will always honor _____ by preferring her needs over your own.

May the Lord bless you with a love for His Word, His Truth and with a heart to pray for your wife and children.

May the Lord bless you with courage, boldness and strength of character to establish godly boundaries and activities that will bless and nurture your loved ones.

May the Lord bless you and _____ with a child of your union and may the generational blessings that have flowed through our family continue to flow through you.

May the Lord bless you with good parenting skills and the wisdom required to be a godly father. May you be a good listener and never tire of blessing your children with quality time, words and caring actions.

We commit to love and pray for you and your family, to be there whenever you need us. We bless this new stage in your life when you cleave to your wife and your parents become your friends.

To our daughter-in-law:

_____ we welcome you into the _____ family. We bless this day of "New Beginnings".

Over the past ___ years we have come to know you as a friend and we love you and cherish you.

You are physically beautiful & radiant today. We bless the beauty of your heart and your soul as well.

We bless you as our daughter-in-law and our friend. We bless you as a bride and rejoice with you as the two of you have vowed before God to love, honor and cherish one another all the days of your lives.

May your marriage relationship be filled with all God's good and perfect gifts that He has in mind for you both.

We bless you as a wife. May the Lord give you unconditional love, patience, wisdom, strength and discernment for the journey that lies ahead of you.

May your relationship with _____grow stronger and sweeter and even more precious as you purpose in your heart to honor God and your husband.

May the Lord prosper you and _____and give you favor with your employers, your family and bless you with godly friends.

We commit to love you and pray for you and to be there whenever you need us or ask for our help.

May the Lord bless you with a home, a place that has space and room to live, grow and play. _____we rejoice over you and celebrate with you.

25th Wedding Anniversary Blessing

This Blessing was given by Terry & Melissa Bone to a husband and wife who reached their 25th anniversary shortly after the both came to know Jesus Christ as their Saviour

Our lives are a story , written by the hand of God.

Truly God knows how the last chapter will end before the first chapter begins.

"_____ and _____, your story so far has included many years of God's unseen hand leading and guiding you even before you recognized his involvement in your lives.

Then, having met Him personally, you discovered the joy of watching God fill in the blanks of your life story – the experience of looking back and recognizing God's sure hand of guidance.

"You have learned to honor God - not out of fear but out of love and respect for His ways in your life. And He has already answered many of your prayers.

"We rejoice in what He has done in your lives and we stand with you at this juncture as you say 'so far so good'.

"You are about to enter the 'time of your lives'. For the number twenty-five is perhaps more significant than just a milestone to mark along the way – more than just a flag we wave above our marriage to prove we have 'above average ability to endure'

"I looked up the number 25 in the Bible to see what, if any mention there might be.

I discovered that no less than FIVE Kings of Israel began their ministry at the age of 25 years. (2 Chronicles 25:1, 27:1, 29:1, 36:5 and 2 Kings 14:2). And each of them were good kings! It seems that God feels that 25 years is often what it takes to mature people for future service. One of those kings was a man named Jotham. His name means "God is perfect" literally complete and pure. The Bible uses the following words to describe Jotham's reign;

"Jotham grew powerful because he walked steadfastly before the Lord his God." (2 Chronicles 27:6)

"The Hebrew phrase in this verse translated 'grew powerful' can mean any of the following:

- to prevail, to become strong or firm
- to be courageous, to be resolute
- to cure, help, repair, fortify

"This is our blessing to you today – May you be like King Jotham in every way:

- in his name - may you never lose sight of the fact that God's ways are complete in your life
- may you walk steadfastly – never to be moved from the confidence of what you know to be true
- may you grow powerfully so that – you prevail in every trial. Become strong through every test, be courageous in every danger, become firm in your understanding, never stubborn but resolute in your commitment to each other
- may your lives and especially your marriage be what causes others to acquire hope and to become strong and be fortified
- may your words and your actions help to cure and repair broken lives, introducing them to their Saviour and Guide
- may your children know their God because of the demonstration of His faithfulness in your lives "

This blessing was followed by a time of prayer

A Retirement Blessing
Based upon Proverbs 31:23

In Biblical times, people worked in the fields outside the city and came inside the gates at night for protection. Upon 'retirement' from regular labor, seniors were often asked to 'sit in the gates' as a sign of honor and to keep watch over the affairs of the city.

Interesting to note: In Old Testament times, Levites (who looked after the temple) were commanded to cease regular labor at fifty years of age and to begin mentoring the newly appointed twenty-five year old Levites (Numbers 8:23-26).

Today we honor your _____ years of labor/service in _____.

We bless your transition from laboring in your chosen field to 'sitting in the gates'.

May this gift of time become an opportunity for continual personal growth.

May you always be a good steward of your time.

May you find purpose and fulfillment in your new and different role in life.

May others seek you for your wisdom.

May you become a mentor to younger men/women in the same profession.

May you always be held in honor by your family and peers.

A Blessing for Senior Parents
Written by the children of Christian parents

In Proverbs 31:28, the children of the virtuous woman rise up to call her blessed.

We want to take this opportunity to honor and bless you for your character and virtuous deeds throughout your life.

(For added effect, those speaking the blessing, can begin in a seated position and stand to their feet as they begin the next sentence)
Today we rise up and call you blessed...

We honor you for the years of selfless service spent in raising your children; for providing for our material, emotional and spiritual needs.

We honor you for preferring our needs over your own and for the sacrifices you made for our sake.

We honor your commitment to following the Lord Jesus and bless you for imparting your spiritual values to us.

We honor you for providing Godly role model(s) to follow. We are blessed and inspired by your integrity.

We thank you for your many prayers that have guarded us from unseen troubles.

We thank you for imparting your wisdom and teaching us valuable life lessons.

We thank you for being available for us in the following ways ... *(at this point in the blessing a couple of brief stories were shared).*

For the remaining years that God grants you to remain upon earth:

May you never be without the presence of the Holy Spirit,

May your heart always be at peace,

May your mind always be alert and learning,

May your strength match the length of your days,

May God keep you in His love at all times.

We bless your memories that you may recall the goodness of God and the great times had with family and friends.

We bless your spiritual life, that you may continue to worship God in spirit and in truth

We commit ourselves to walk with you for the rest of your journey on earth.

During the sunset years of your life, as you become less able to care for yourselves, we will become more available to help look after your needs. (or if separated by distance – to visit when we are able and to pray for you when we cannot be near you).

As you look upon your children today, you are also looking at the beginning of a legacy that will last for generations.

We commit ourselves to carry forward your legacy and pass on our spiritual heritage to our children and grandchildren.

Finish with the Aaronic blessing

House Blessing

"Every good and perfect gift is from above, coming down from the Father of the heavenly lights..." (James 1:17 NIV).

A House Dedication is an act of gratitude and recognition that God is the source and sustainer of all good things.

"We bless this house as a good and perfect gift from God our Father. It is God's choice for our family both in structure and in location. We bless the neighborhood and the relationships we shall form while living here."

A House Dedication is an act of consecration – inviting the presence of God's Spirit to dwell with the family in this home.

"We bless this house , that it may be a dwelling place of the Holy Spirit whom we now invite to dwell among us, to guard us guide us, teach us and convict us when we stray from the path of honor and family blessing.

"We declare the cornerstone of this house to be Jesus Christ. (read 1 Peter 4:2-8)".

A House Dedication is an act of Protection - It is an acknowledgement that God will be the Protector of this family and their home against those forces that rob their peace or possessions. It is a request to keep the structure and its occupants safe from fire and other dangers.

"Father God we ask for your protection upon this home. Set your angels to guard the four corners of this property. May there never be any unauthorized access. May nothing ever be taken or stolen from this house. May you keep us safe at all times when dwelling here.

"May this home always be a place of peaceful refuge fro the storms of life for every occupant, both family members and visitors."

(The participants may also wish to anoint the doorposts with oil in the main entranceway and to walk and pray through every room in the house).

Tools of the Trade

SECTION C

Additional Resources

The Bible

Prayer

Media resources

The Bible will help you craft a blessing

Some passages of scripture, such as Psalm 128 were actually written as blessings. Hundreds more are phrased in such a way as to be easily incorporated into a written or spoken blessing.... Below is a small sample just to get you started. Don't stop with these. Look for more scriptures on many more topics as you read the Bible yourself.

Blessings in Christ	Ephesians 1:3
Chosen by God	Ephesians 1:4,11
Obedience and Long Life	Deut. 5:33 , 30:19,20
Rewards for Kindness	Ruth 2:12
For a Child to Prosper	1 Kings 2:1-3
Family Blessing	Psalm 128
The 'marriage bed'	Proverbs 5:18-19
Fertility	Genesis 24:60, Deut. 28:11
Prosperity in Business	Deut. 28:1-8, 12-15
Financial Blessing	Deut. 15:10, Psalm 37:25-26, Prov. 19:17, 22:9
Tithing	Malachi 3:10-11
Physical Health	3 John 1
Peace and Holiness	1 Thessalonians 5:23
Wisdom and Revelation	Ephesians 1:17
Wisdom	Proverbs 3:12-18
Spiritual Insight	Ephesians 1:18-19
Spiritual Power	Ephesians 3:15-19
Blessings in Trials	Matthew 5:4,10,11
Spiritual Hunger & Humility	Matthew 5:3,5-9

The Role of Prayer

A blessing is not the same as a prayer , yet prayer plays an important role in releasing blessing in people's lives. The enemy of our souls will try to counter the effect of spoken blessing through various means. Prayers spoken with faith and accuracy are able to condition the spiritual atmosphere around those we love, making it easier for them to believe and receive God's provision in every aspect of their lives. If blessings are 'packages' being delivered to the door of a person's heart, then your prayers can help to clear any spiritual 'traffic jams' between heaven and the life of the one you love! A sample prayer of protection follows:

Daily Declaration Prayer for my family

"Heavenly Father I bring my family <name them one by one> before you.

Today I declare in the name of Jesus that my children <and ...> are under Your protection, direction, and when necessary, Your correction.

I place them under the protection and blessing of my believing prayers.

In every choice that confronts them , I declare that they will receive wisdom to understand the righteous path and the receive the grace to choose that path even if they have not been seeking it.

Keep them from all accident, injury and illness.

Lead them away from temptation and trial except for the ones you have specifically sent for their growth and for their good.

Fill them with your Spirit and passion for You. Drain from their soul any love for the world and the things of the world. Give them a spirit of wisdom and understanding in every aspect of their lives.

I declare that no thing, no obstacle or circumstance will prevent them from moving toward their destiny today. Amen"

Additional Media Resources

The Power of Blessing Book and DVD Series
Available through our website:
www.powerofblessing.com

Children's Ministry Resources
Available through our website:
www.powerofblessing.com

The Family Blessing, *by Rolf Garborg*
White Stone Books, Lakeland Florida, USA.
www.whitestonebooks.com

The Ancient Paths, *by Craig Hill*
Family Foundations Publishing, Littleton Colorado, USA.
www.familyfoundations.com

Emotionally Free, *by Dr. Grant Mullen*
This and other resources available at:
www.drgrantmullen.com

The Blessing, *by Gary Smalley & John Trent*
Pocket Books, New York , N.Y., USA
www.SimonSays.com

The Name Book, *by Dorothy Astoria,*
1997 Bethany House Publishers.

Bar Barakah, A Parent's Guide to a Christian Bar Mitzvah, Family foundations Int. (FFI)
Same contact info as Ancient Paths